75 TOP CAR MUSEUMS
IN EUROPE & AMERICA

Also by Michael Milne

Roadster Guide to America's Classic Car Museums & Attractions

Philadelphia Liberty Trail: Trace the Path of America's Heritage
(co-author with Larissa Milne)

75 Top Car Museums in Europe & America

A Collection of Magazine Articles

FIRST EDITION

MICHAEL MILNE

CHANGES IN LONGITUDE PRESS
WWW.CHANGESINLONGITUDE.COM

Thank you to all the editors who have published my stories and the museum curators who have answered my endless questions with patience.

.

Contents

EUROPE

Bulgaria	Cars of Socialism Museum	1
Denmark	Skoda Museum	4
France	Cite de' L'Automobile	6
	Manoir de'l'Automobile	9
	24 Hours of Le Mans Museum	13
Germany	Dr. Carl Benz Auto Museum	17
	Mercedes-Benz Museum	20
	Porsche Museum	23
	Technik Museums Sinsheim	26
	Technik Museums Speyer	26
	Trabi Museum	30
Greece	Hellenic Motor Museum	33
Italy	Alfa Romeo Historical Museum	36
	Fiat Museum	40
	National Auto Museum	44
	Museo Enzo Ferrari	48
	Museo Ferrari	48
	Museo Lamborghini	48
	Collezione Umberto Panini Motor Museum	48
	State Police Car Museum	51
Poland	Museum of Municipal Engineering	54
Romania	Tiriac Collection	58
Slovenia	Technical Museum of Slovenia	61

UK	Haynes International Motor Museum	64
	London Bus Museum at Brooklands	67
	London Transport Museum	67
	National Motor Museum at Beaulieu	71
	National Museum of Scotland	74
	Riverside Museum	74

NORTH AMERICA

Canada	Gasoline Alley	80
	Jim's Vintage Garages	85
	Manitoba Antique Automobile Museum	85
USA		

East	AACA Museum, PA	89
	Boyertown Museum of Historic Vehicles, PA	93
	Classic Motor Museum, MD	96
	Crawford Auto Aviation Collection, OH	99
	National Packard Museum, OH	99
	America's Packard Museum, OH	99
	Ford Piquette Avenue Plant, MI	103
	Frick Car & Carriage Museum, PA	107
	Gilmore Car Museum, MI	110
	Henry Ford Museum of American Innovation, MI	114
	Heritage Museums & Gardens, MA	117
	Keystone Truck & Tractor Museum, PA	120
	National Museum of the United States Army, VA	124
	Simeone Foundation Automotive Museum, PA	129
	Tampa Bay Automobile Museum, FL	134
	US Army Transportation Museum, VA	138
	Wheels of Yesteryear, SC	142

Central	Auburn Cord Duesenberg Museum, IN	145
	Early Ford V8 Foundation, IN	145
	National Auto & Truck Museum, IN	145

Indianapolis Motor Speedway Museum, IN   150
Lane Motor Museum, TN   153
Midwest Dream Car Collection, KS   158
Midwest Microcar Museum, WI   162
National Corvette Museum, KY   166
Pontiac-Oakland Museum, IL   170
Presley Motors at Graceland, TN   173
Edge Motor Museum, TN   173
Speedwell Museum of American Speed, NE   176
Stahl's Automotive Foundation, MI   180
Studebaker National Museum, IN   184
Wisconsin Automobile Museum, WI   188

West   Cussler Museum, CO   192
Franklin Auto Museum, AZ   196
LeMay – America's Car Museum, WA   199
LeMay Family Collection, WA   199
Mullin Automobile Museum, CA   204
Murphy Auto Museum, CA   204
National Automobile Museum & Shelby   209
    Heritage Center, NV
Petersen Automotive Museum, CA   213
Rambler Ranch, CO   217
Route 66 Electric Vehicle Museum, AZ   221
Unser Racing Museum, NM   224
War Eagles Air Museum, NM   228
Western Antique Aeroplane & Automobile
Museum, OR   232
Zimmerman Automobile Driving Museum, CA   236

INTERVIEWS   In The Garage With Jay Leno   239
    On the Road with Alice Cooper   243
INDEX   247

ABOUT THE AUTHOR   250

INTRODUCTION

This book is an in-depth look at some of my favorite car museums in Europe and North America. It's a collection of articles I've written for *Hemmings Motor News*, *Classic & Sports Car*, *Octane*, *Military History Vehicle*, *AAA World*, *Classic Motorsports*, the *Philadelphia Inquirer*, and other publications.

I've also included my interviews with car collectors Jay Leno and Alice Cooper.

Hope to see you somewhere down the road.

Michael Milne

EUROPE

BULGARIA

BEING SOCIAL IN BULGARIA

CARS OF SOCIALISM MUSEUM Peshtera

You know you're in a former Eastern Bloc country when a giant portrait of Vladimir Lenin consumes one wall of a car museum. Such is the case at the Cars Of Socialism Museum in Peshtera, Bulgaria, about a two-hour drive southeast of the capital of Sofia. Established in 2016, the museum is tucked inside a former movie theater at the Hotel Heat.

The collection reaches beyond cars to highlight what life was like behind the Iron Curtain during the Cold War. The signs are all in Bulgarian, which uses the Cyrillic alphabet, but a visitor can still get a flavor for life, both automotive and otherwise, from 1945 to 1989.

Visitors descend a grand staircase with a striking view of the surprisingly colorful two-dozen car collection. Directly opposite, several Cold War era cars sit on the former stage, perched in front of a mural of Sofia's Ulitsa Saborna, so the cars appear as if they are on a grand old European boulevard. Old Bulgarian pop music blares out of loudspeakers, lending a surrealistic tone to the setting.

The perimeter of the room is devoted to artifacts and ephemera of daily life under communism, but cars take center stage. The Soviet-built 1970 GAZ M21 Volga, with its leaping deer hood ornament, was considered an upscale vehicle that was favored by, well, those in favor. (Note: the museum does not display the exact model year of each car. Since models didn't change as frequently as in the West, it can be difficult to date certain models. Museum representative Dinko Kushev provided the years for each car.)

A light blue 1965 ZAZ 965 (not to be confused with GAZ above), with an air-cooled, rear-mounted engine, was a ubiquitous Ukrainian-built car that "borrowed" design cues from the Fiat 600 and was the Soviet Union's answer to the popular Volkswagen Beetle. (ZAZ is an acronym for the Zaporozhets Automobile Building Plant in the Ukrainian "Motor City" of Zaporizhzhia.)

Fiats were widespread behind the Iron Curtain; millions of them were manufactured for decades in Poland. A flaming orange 1985-1987 Polski Fiat 126p rear-engine hatchback is a prime example of the diminutive people mover.

The 1988 Moskvich 412/2140 sedan, with the whisper of a tail fin, was the result of an interesting partnership between Bulgaria and the USSR. The Soviets shipped knock-down kits to Bulgaria, where they were then assembled. The cars were known for their bright colors; the example here is tomato red. (Note that some model numbers listed here varied based on where the car was sold.)

Any debate about the different political systems in the two Germanys could be settled by a comparison between West German marques like Mercedes, BMW, and Audi with the East German Trabant. The oft-maligned "Trabi" came to symbolize manufacturing quality (or lack thereof) in a planned economy – yet people waited years for one of these "toasters on wheels." A powder blue 1988 Trabant 601S station wagon on display sports a pair of tail fins; this racy design feature appeared after fins had gone out of style in the West.

Another East German beauty is the 1963 Wartburg 311. (The three-digit designation, starting with a "3," was a holdover from the plant's pre-war days as a BMW factory in eastern Germany that was later appropriated by the victorious Soviet army.) The two-toned lemon and cream colors make it a surprising confection in the bland surroundings for which it was produced. Based on an older design, it was already out of date when it premiered.

Other Eastern European car manufacturers represented here include Warsawa (Poland), Lada (USSR), and Zastava (Yugoslavia). There are also Renaults that were assembled in the Bulgarian city of Plovdiv from 1967 through 1970.

Items on display from daily life range from plastic black-and-white televisions, to a Soviet-themed version of the board game *Battleship* and automotive trading cards. There's an extensive collection of Matchbox cars, manufactured in Bulgaria under license in the 1980s. Considering the prosaic cars he would have seen on the streets, one wonders what thoughts went through the head of a Bulgarian boy when he played with a toy Firebird Trans Am.

No exhibit of Communist-era memorabilia is complete without signs and banners exhorting the masses to pull together and work harder for the motherland. The walls of the museum are full of such vintage messages. We could loosely translate one, which urged workers to "meet the new agricultural plan with the wonderful tools provided to them." (They appeared to be ordinary shovels.) It was interesting to watch Bulgarians who lived through that period pointing and laughing as they read the signs. It makes one wonder if they were silently laughing at them all along.

Cars of Socialism Museum 56 Mihail Takev Street, Peshtera, Bulgaria
www.CarsOfSocialism.com

DENMARK

Czech Mate in Denmark

Škoda Museum Glamsbjerg

The Czech automotive industry has often been lost in the shadow of its German neighbor. However, Czech car production is one of the oldest in Europe. Škoda's predecessor company, Laurin & Klement, started producing cars in 1905; Tatra built its first car in 1897. During the 1920s and 1930s Czech cars, Tatra in particular, were making great strides in technology. Today Škoda still produces vehicles under the ownership of Volkswagen and Tatra manufactures trucks and military vehicles.

Once upon a time, Danish car aficionados Ole Hansen, his son Jan, and Carsten Andersen decided to start a car museum devoted to their favorite marque. They opened the Škoda Museum in 1999 and moved it to this location in a fairy tale looking barn in 2001.

During our visit, the 75-year-old Ole, whose flowing white hair and beard give him a gnome-like appearance that adds to the enchanted setting of the museum, guided us through a timeline of 35 Škoda vehicles. He doesn't speak much English and our Danish is (very) limited, so museum member Fin Mathiesen translated.

When asked why there's a museum devoted to Czech cars in Denmark, Ole shrugs and says, "I'm crazy. Since 1962 I worked on Škoda when my father started a dealership. In Denmark a Škoda was a cheap car in the '60s and '70s. A little cheaper than a Volkswagen Beetle, so they were popular."

All the cars in the collection, some of which are on loan, can drive. The oldest car here is a 1937 Škoda 420 Popular. The value-priced line was exported as far afield as China. A Cold War era 1953 Škoda 973 Army Radiovan had a wood burning stove in the rear to provide heat for the soldiers. Not surprisingly, only thirty were produced with this nifty feature.

But all was not bleak behind the Iron Curtain, the flame red 1958 Škoda 450 Roadster wouldn't have looked out of place with Dustin Hoffman driving it in The Graduate. According to the sales brochure it could reach 84 mph on its 50 hp 4-cylinder engine. The 1972 Škoda 110/120 was a one-off prototype police car with a "souped up" 85 hp engine, which does make you wonder just what they were chasing.

To prove the sturdiness of the marque, a 1982 Škoda (nicknamed Oda) completed the 2015 Mongol Rally, more than 10,000 rugged miles from the historic Goodwood Circuit in England to Ulaanbaatar, Mongolia. For good measure, after the race it even drove back to Denmark.

Other Škodas on display include a 1960 Octavia, a rare 1969 1000 MBX, and a 1997 Felicia LXi; the first model that Volkswagen, who started taking over Škoda in 1991, had a hand in.

Skoda Museum Nårupvej 32, DK-5620 Glamsbjerg, Denmark
www.skodamuseum.dk

FRANCE

FRENCH REVOLUTIONS:
LUXURY MARQUES, RACERS AND MORE

CITÉ DE L'AUTOMOBILE MUSÉE NATIONAL – SCHLUMPF COLLECTION
Mulhouse

It's not every car museum that will let you sit in a vehicle and flip it in a 360-degree barrel roll only yards away from a rare and valuable Bugatti. But that's the kind of variety to expect at the Cité de l'Automobile Musée National – Schlumpf Collection, located in Mulhouse, France, just ten miles from the Rhine River and German border. More than 400 vehicles are on display, with an emphasis on rare and prestigious European marques. Descriptive placards are in French, German, and English.

The museum is divided into three main areas: 1) Motorcar Masterpieces, the most luxurious cars from the 1930s, including several Bugattis; 2) The Motorcar Experience, representing the history of the automobile from 1878 through today; and 3) Motor Racing. With a floor size of more than a quarter million square feet, trams are also available to whisk visitors among the exhibits. In addition, out back there is a racing track where, for an extra fee, visitors can zip around in vintage sports cars. Among the dozen choices are a 1957 Bentley S1, 1959 Jaguar XK150 and, somewhat incongruously, a 1965 Chevy Impala.

Avid car collector, Fritz Schlumpf, along with his brother Hans, was a Swiss-born local textile manufacturer. In 1976, he set up the car collection in an old brick factory. Around the same time, their business enterprises ran into financial difficulties and they had to shut down. The collection might have remained hidden from both creditors and the world. But the following year local union officials seeking company assets discovered it and laid siege to the building while the Schlumpf brothers sought refuge in their villa nearby.

The brothers were sent back to Switzerland while the collection remained, soon to become a very visible public asset and tourist attraction. While the brothers never did get their cars back, the authorities eventually added the Schlumpf name to the museum. Their loss is the public's gain as, rather than being sold off piecemeal, this incredible collection is still on view for car buffs.

A tour of the museum reveals that Fritz Schlumpf enjoyed exquisite taste in collecting and restoring cars. Start out in the Motorcar Masterpieces room. Here, overhead lighting is dimmed, and cars are showcased by tiny spotlights to augment their jewel-like appearance. The star of the show is the 1929 Bugatti Royale Coupé Napoleon Type 41 with its massive 12.7 liter 8-cylinder engine. Once the most expensive car in the world, it was Ettore Bugatti's personal vehicle. Designed to be driven by kings, only six of the stretch-hooded vehicles were ever produced. Nearby is a 1933 Bugatti Royale Type 41 limousine that was purchased as part of a bulk sale from noted American Bugatti collector John W. Shakespeare in 1964.

Next, step into the main museum concourse, which is brightly lit with cars lined up chronologically in long rows. Anchoring the first row is an 1893 Peugeot Phaetonnet Type 8 boasting a two-cylinder engine that cranked out a mere three horsepower. Perhaps the 1905 Mercedes Double-Phaeton Type 28/50 was the origin of the term "back seat driver." The car's great weight made it so difficult to stop that there was an additional brake in the rear for a passenger to employ.

Daily drivers are also part of the collection including a 1939 Peugeot Berline Type 202; West German 1967 NSU Ro 80 (its Wankel engine was unreliable); and a 1969 Simca Berline Type 100. The latter is not often seen in museums; I only recognized it because my parents drove one (which was an odd sight in 1960s Ohio).

Just when you think you've seen it all, turn a corner to the Motor Racing section, where dozens of race cars lined up in pairs looked poised for the starting flag in an area the size of several NBA basketball courts. A pair of 2009 and 2010 Renault F1 cars lead the way, followed by classic racers like a 1953 Gordini 23S, 1957 Maserati 250 F, and a 1963 Lotus Type 33.

The Cité de l'Automobile is very hands-on for visitors. Engage in an actual rollover by strapping into a late model Peugeot (there's a factory nearby that offers tours) or try to hand-crank a 1923 Citroën Torpedo; the latter endeavor makes one appreciate the advent of the electric starter. In the engine display, press a button to hear the distinctive roar of Bugatti engines while watching a video of their schematics. A collection of animal-themed radiator cap mascots and dozens of toy cars are a hit with younger visitors.

Cité de l'Automobile National Museum – Schlumpf Collection
17 Rue de la Mertzau, 68100 Mulhouse, France
www.citedelautomobile.com/en

To the Manoir Born:
Vintage Autos in the French Countryside

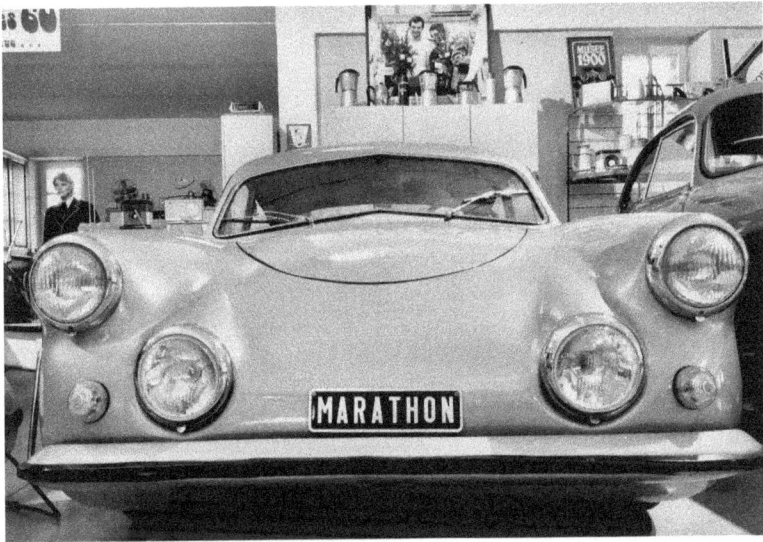

Manoir de l'Automobile et des Vieux Métiers Brittany

After motoring across rolling pastures dotted with livestock, the namesake stone manor of the Manoir de l'Automobile et des Vieux Métiers (Manor of the Automobile and Old Trades) rises Oz-like in the Breton countryside of France. Here, in a 17th-century mansion, more than 400 vehicles representing a century of motoring heritage are on view.

When classic car connoisseur Michel Hommell acquired the farm more than three decades ago, it consisted of dilapidated old buildings stuffed with cows, pigs, and chickens. But the Lorraine native had been buying old vehicles since he was 18 and dreamt of transforming the property into a magnificent automotive showpiece.

As a visit reveals, his dream came true. Adjacent to the museum is the Circuit de Lohéac, the oldest Rallycross circuit in France.

The sprawling museum is divided into more than a dozen themed salons – highlights include the Lamborghini Room; Enzo Ferrari Room; Amphibious Cars; Peugeot; GT Room; and the F1 Starting Grid featuring 18 Formula 1 cars poised for the red starting lights to extinguish.

Cars in the Hall of Ancestors like the oldest vehicle in the museum, an 1899 De Dion Bouton, are referred to as clunkers. Other old road warriors include a few cycle cars like the 1922 Amilcar, 1924 Benjamin and 1924 Mathis Type P.

Italian Jobs

To many, the rooms devoted to the output of Lamborghini and Ferrari host the pinnacle of automotive styling. What's not to love about the sinewy curves of a 12-cylinder 370 hp 1970 Lamborghini Miura S, whose forerunner wowed the crowd at the Turin Auto Show. Or stroll over to the Enzo Ferrari room to gaze upon a 1978 BB (Berlinetta Boxer) 512 Carburettor. Its mid-mounted flat engine was a competitive response to the Miura.

The French Collection

Naturally, in a French motor museum, native brand Peugeot is well represented. Highlights of the Peugeot collection include a 1935 601 Roadster with its sleek aerodynamic shape, a 1938 302 Cabriolet and a 1936 402 Eclipse with a retractable hardtop hood that slides into the trunk.

French panache is evident in several homegrown autos. The sporty 1953 Marathon Corsaire coupe, with a two-cylinder rear-mounted Boxer engine, was the product of a short-lived venture that was supposed to compete with Porsche. While the sleek tomato-red two-cylinder 1958 U.M.A.P. (short for L'Usine Moderne d'Application Plastique," or as we say in English, plastic) was a revolutionary mini grand tourer with a fiberglass body.

One of the most unusual cars anywhere is the 1957 Velam Corse. The diminutive bathtub-shaped Velam is a one-off single-seat roadster that looks like a toy that was just opened on Christmas morning. The 12-hp engine powered it to a 24-hour record in its class of 68 average mph.

Other French marques range from the well-known to the obscure including Renault, Facel Vega, Matra, René Bonnet, Alpine, Autobleu, Tracta, Mathis, Léon Bollée, UMAP and Marathon.

Water, Water Everywhere

Cars that can also motor through the water are often overlooked but that's not the case here with a group of unusual models from the mid-century, when the ability to drive a car into water seemed all the rage. At least the 1942 jeep was built for practical purposes, there was a war on after all. Others include a 1952 Voisin, 1961 Amphicar and a 1942 Hydromobile.

Daily Drivers

The many comments written in response to a recent story on the Hemmings website showed that plenty of classic car buffs would love to see more regular cars in museums. They've come to the right place here. Despite all the high-brow metal, the Manoir de l'Automobile is not afraid to display more pedestrian vehicles that are often ignored in the museum world. Hence, you'll find a 1958 Vespa 400 ACMA (automobile, not scooter), 1954 Simca and a 1961 Simca Aronde Ranch. Oddities include a 1974 Citroën Pony light utility vehicle that was produced under license in Greece by Namco and a 1989 Trabant from East Germany rigged up for motor racing. Hard to believe, but there is a whole subculture devoted to racing these oft belittled, but now much beloved, products from the Cold War. Another potential racer is the 1965 Ford Cortina Lotus Mk1 in eye-catching white with green side flashes.

Gentlemen, Start Your Engines

Naturally, a museum adjacent to a racing circuit showcases speed. The newest addition to the Manor, the F1 Starting Grid, was added in 1999 and holds 18 race cars poised for ignition. Among them are a 1980 McLaren M29, 1983 Ferrari 126 C3 and a 1996 Williams Renault driven by Jacques Villenueve in his debut Formula 1 year.

About three hours into your visit, right about when you're ready to grab a cider and crepe in the on-site café, one more salon in the garret beckons. Devoted to Rally Cross and Small Sport, a small sampling of this area includes a 1997 Ford Escort WRC, 1990 Citroen BX and a car built by a fledgling company started by the museum's owner, a 1998 Hommell Cabster.

An unusual section of the museum may provide respite for those in your group who don't fancy spending hours ogling classic cars. In the Old Trades area re-creations of twenty stores and workshops representing old village life have been filled with antiques and period-clothed mannequins featuring bygone crafts like hat making and butchering. Elsewhere, the Hall of Models holds several thousand scale model cars displayed in glass cases and spot lit like shiny baubles for sale at Tiffany. Among the miniatures I finally found a Bugatti I could afford.

Manoir de l'Automobile 4 Rue de la Cour Neuve, 35550 Loheac, France
www.manoir-automobile.fr/home

ALL IN A DAY'S WORK:
THE 24 HOURS AT LE MANS MUSEUM

24 HOURS OF LE MANS MUSEUM Le Mans

To many, there is no greater spectacle in motor racing than the 24 Hours at Le Mans. In 2019, it even crossed over into the mainstream with the global success of the film *Ford vs Ferrari*. For those who can't make it to this sterling event, the 24 Hours of Le Mans Museum, located trackside, is a worthy substitute. The museum was founded in 1961 by Automobile Club Ouest and moved to its current location 30 years later.

The 140-vehicle collection tells the history of motor racing in the Sarthe department of France with particular emphasis on the heralded 24-hour race. Legendary marques include Jaguar, Ford, Ferrari, Bentley, Porsche, Matra, and more.

The spacious museum isn't just a monument to racing, however; it's also a worthy classic car museum too. A non-racing display includes Veteran Cars with significant local history while focusing on French automotive heritage and technology.

Visitors start out with a stroll through the Le Mans Hall of Fame where such luminaries as Ettore Bugatti, the Bentley Boys and six-time winner Jacky Ickx, who, in 1969 famously walked to his car in protest of the dangerous sprinting start, are honored.

Ickx was making a point about lax safety protocols at the race. According to former racer Hervé Guyomard, who managed the circuit for four decades starting in 1970 and is now a guide at the museum, "Racing was very dangerous in those years. I had many friends killed."

One of the oldest racing vehicles in the collection is the 1924 Bentley Torpédo Van den Plas. When Walter Bentley heard about the still fairly new race one of its attractions was that, unlike nighttime bans in England at the time, racing was permitted at night. Powered with a 3-liter Red Label motor generating 82 bhp, drivers John Duff and Franck Clément won the race, achieving great fame for the Bentley marque.

During our visit, in a sight familiar to any owner of a classic car, the house mechanics had taken apart a 1927 Tracta Gephi with pieces strewn on the ground. According to Guyomard, "For me this is the most important car in the museum. It was a pioneer in the principle of front-wheel drive that has saved millions of lives." The car also participated in the 1929 race.

With its Lilliputian size, the 1935 Simca 5 Gordini looks like it would be right at home at the Dodgem bumper car ride at Brighton Pier, which is not surprising since it is the smallest car with the smallest engine (4-cylinder, 568 cc, 30 bhp) in Le Mans history. Not surprisingly it won its class, most likely because it was the only competitor in it. In the post-war years Amédée Gordini went on to racing history with Renault.

In a museum chock full of sleek racers, it's difficult to stand out, but one car manages to do so. The 1952 Socéma Gregoire is a one-off prototype of an aircraft gas turbine engine mated with an aerodynamically smooth rocket-shaped aluminum body. Despite being capable of 200 mph speeds, the car was never able to overcome cost and braking issues.

Ford's upending of Ferrari's dominance in the mid-Sixties has become the stuff of both real-life and cinematic legend. The 1967 Ford GT 40 on view here stopped a bit short of this achievement when a blown head gasket forced it out of the '67 race in the 14th hour.

Guyomard lovingly admires it and notes, "The GT 40 was the last car of one pleasing shape, without wings and aerodynamics. It's very pleasant to drive." It's also a powerful example of the successful British-American effort to beat Ferrari.

As Guyomard ruefully points out, the shape of cars was on the cusp of change. One example of the newfangled automotive architecture is the 1974 Matra Simca 670 B V12, it represents a pinnacle of French motoring success as it completed a three-year sweep by the French marque at Le Mans.

From a design standpoint, Audi started taking things to a new level. Its 2002 winning R8 FSI and 2013 winning Audi E-tron Quattro R118H hybrid diesel-electric look like they were purloined from the set of a *Robocop* film.

However, since there are multiple categories in the race, the racers aren't all maximum horsepower and speed. The petite 1950 Renault 4 CV, with its 4-cylinder engine pushing it to 66 mph took on Le Mans that same year, leaving only after an accident in the 17th hour, having covered 92 laps. It's considered by many to be a prime example of a post-war austerity racer.

The area around the city of Le Mans was also a hotbed of transportation innovation. The Veteran section of the museum includes many vehicles produced by local manufacturers, including a 1901 Amédée Bollée Fils Type D Limousine and an 1897 Vis à Vis built by former Bollée employee Henri Vallée, one of only 15 produced.

Other Veterans of historic significance include a 1900 Panhard & Levassor Type A2 Phaéton, powered by a Daimler "Phenix" 2-cylinder engine, and a French-built 1908 Krieger Électrique A155 front-wheel drive electric bus; many of these saw action as ambulances during World War I.

Scale model fans will enjoy an impressive display. Hundreds of models represent the entries for each race, with the top three occupying pride of place on their own miniature podium.

You'll also want to stroll the circuit of the legendary race. As you pass under the iconic mammoth Dunlop tire embedded in the ground, you can almost hear the roar of past winners crossing the finish line. Stop at museum reception for a self-guided tour pamphlet.

One of the joys of driving to the 24 Hours of Le Mans Museum is motoring along some of the very same rural roadways that are used in the race. For a moment, even the most sedate bloke driving a rental car Peugeot can feel like they are Derek Hill careening around a curve in the waning hours of the race.

For those in your group who may not want to spend hours ogling the glories of racing cars, the city of Le Mans itself provides a pleasant diversion. The Old City boasts one of the finest examples of fortified Roman walls anywhere, along with sights related to the birthplace of the Plantagenet dynasty. Drop them off there first before motoring away to relive the glories of the 24 Hours at Le Mans.

24 Hours of Le Mans Museum 9 Place Luigi Chinetti, 72100 Le Mans, France
www.lemans-musee24h.com/en

GERMANY

Dr. Benz and the Bertha of the First Road Trip

Dr. Carl Benz Auto Museum Ladenberg

After the invention of the automobile, it didn't take long for the discovery of one of the best uses for the new-fangled contraption: road trip! Both facets come together at the Dr. Carl Benz Auto Museum in Ladenburg, Germany. The first car came courtesy of Dr. Benz himself, while the first road trip was a product of his intrepid wife, Bertha.

Nestled in a residential neighborhood, the 70-car museum occupies an unassuming tan brick structure that was the original automotive manufacturing facility of C. Benz Sons, where production began in 1906. (Note: While Benz spelled his first name with a "K," when he set up C. Benz Sons he used a "C.")

The building holds an incredible spot in motoring heritage. The bones of its former factory days, when Benz churned out 300 chassis here, are evident: the entire roof is a saw-toothed skylight, while the solid walls are mere supports for oversize windows that let in sun and fresh air for the workers. Exposed girders overhead and the sweet smell of motor oil complete the industrial tableau.

Several of the cars on display stand in the very production hall where they were manufactured. One of them is a 1924 Benz 8/25 that was discovered abandoned in a shed. It's one of the last two cars built by C. Benz Sons in Ladenburg for Benz's own use; two years later the company merged with Daimler.

The museum is partnered with the Mercedes-Benz Museum in Stuttgart and includes Mercedes-Benz and Maybach cars, as well as other German and European marques.

A baby-blue 1939 Maybach SW 42 convertible is an elegant standout. By contrast, sitting next to it is a 10 horsepower 1926 Hanomag. Known for its resemblance to a loaf of rye bread, it was popular with young people in the 1920s and looks like it could be squeezed into the Maybach's trunk.

A pair of silvery mid-century 4-cylinder roadsters highlights the varied output that were achieved from each: the 1955 Porsche Model 356 cranks out 70 horsepower while the 1957 Mercedes SLR W121 more than doubles it at 148.

Open-wheel racing heritage is also on display, including the French-built 1922 Amilcar CC (with a sporty 27 horsepower engine it was known as the "poor man's Bugatti") and a 1972 Fuchs Formula Super Vee.

In the early days cars were so rare that few people knew how to drive. To overcome this sales obstacle, the price of the 1898 Benz Patent Motorwagen Velo included a driving instructor.

Other attractions at the museum include early bicycles, motorcycles, pre-war Leica cameras, vintage automobilia signs and gas pumps, and, surprisingly, a circa 1908 Sears Motor Buggy.

Despite Benz's success, things weren't so cut and dry when he started out. He married Bertha Benz, a well-educated woman who gave her husband the money to develop the Benz Patent Motor Car. But it's difficult to sell new technology if people aren't convinced it works. That's where Bertha came in, although somewhat surreptitiously.

On my visit a special guest was also touring the facility: Jutta Benz, a retired history teacher, is the great-granddaughter of Karl and Bertha Benz. Born in 1942, she grew up across from the factory. She relayed the story of Bertha's historic first road trip as told to her by her grandfather Eugen, who was one of two brothers taken along by their mother for the ride. The round trip between Mannheim and Pforzheim covered more than 110 miles.

It was August 1888 and according to Jutta, "Bertha was concerned about her investment. Karl hadn't taken the car on a journey to prove it can do it. He was hard-headed and not convinced that people would buy his invention. So, without her husband knowing about it, my great grandma placed her teenaged sons, my grandfather Eugen and great-uncle Richard, in a Model III for a road trip."

"Of course, there were no gas stations back then, so for fuel Bertha stopped at a pharmacy for a solvent that removed spots in clothing. When a fuel line clogged, she cleaned it with a hat pin and when heat made the chain stretch, she took it to a blacksmith to shorten it."

Jutta recalls, "Every time my grandfather told the story it changed a bit, but the main part stayed the same" and the rest is history.

Later, Jutta proved her innate driving chops by taking a replica of the historic car out for a spin around the museum. The Bertha Benz Memorial Route is now marked with historical signs so motorists can relive the world's first road trip. For more information about the road trip go to www.bertha-benz.de and click on the British flag for English.

Dr. Carl Benz Automuseum Ilvesheimer Straße 26, 68526 Ladenburg, Germany
www.automuseum-dr-carl-benz.de

LIKE NO OTHER: THE MERCEDES-BENZ MUSEUM

MERCEDES-BENZ MUSEUM Stuttgart

Janis Joplin's plaintive wail, "Oh Lord, won't you buy me a Mercedes Benz" just wouldn't work with any other vehicle. Not only is the marque descended from the man who is considered the originator of the automobile, Karl Benz, it has also filled car lovers over the years with equal parts envy, longing, and respect. For almost every generation, even counter-culture hippies of the 1960s, the ownership of a Mercedes-Benz has shown the world that you've "made it."

The Mercedes-Benz Museum in Stuttgart, Germany celebrates this storied marque. With its shimmery silver space-age exterior, the structure is as monumental as the brand's image; the central atrium is tall enough for the Statue of Liberty to lower her torch and step right inside. In 2016, the company celebrated 130 years of the automobile and a decade of the museum's existence. Because Benz was the first patent holder for automobiles, the company is the only one that can trace the entire range of the automotive era as part of their own history.

The tour begins on the top floor; pod-like elevators, described as "time machines," whisk visitors back to 1886, when Carl Benz obtained a patent for the world's first automobile, the three-wheeled Benz Patent-Motorwagen. A replica of the pioneering vehicle is on display, the original having been given to the Deutsches Museum in Munich by Mr. Benz himself.

Benz' patent application beat his early rivals, Gottlieb Daimler and Wilhelm Maybach, by only a few months. Their version of an early automobile, an original 1886 Daimler Motorkutsche, paired with its pioneering "Grandfather Clock" engine, sits next to the Benz Patent-Motorwagen.

An 1898 Daimler Motor-Lastwagen is believed to be the oldest surviving delivery truck in the world. In the early days – due to the product they usually conveyed – they were simply called beer wagons. It's unusual due to its side-mounted radiator located below the driver, reflective of the experimentation still occurring in the early days of automotive engineering.

The "Mercedes" brand first came into existence in 1900, named after the daughter of Austrian businessman and auto racer Emil Jellinek. Befitting its exalted status, the world's oldest Mercedes is set on a pedestal here; the 1902 Mercedes-Simplex 40 HP was so called because it was easy to drive. It was a racing car that was bought by American millionaire William K. Vanderbilt who, upon picking it up, raced from Stuttgart straightaway to Paris. It set a speed record of 69 mph but, because this was a different era, there were no amenities like a windshield, doors, headrests or seat belts in the open-air vehicle to coddle the occupants.

Moving forward in time to 1936 reveals the most photographed car in the museum, which is saying a lot since it is competing against more than 150 remarkable autos. The scarlet 1936 Mercedes-Benz

500K Spezial Roadster stands out even among a pack of stellar vehicles and was the apex of the brand during the 1930s.

The walls of the museum are decorated with highlights of world events to reflect the timeline of the vehicles. A vintage photo of a young Elvis Presley can only mean one thing; we're about to set eyes on one of the most popular classic cars of all time: the 1955 Mercedes-Benz 300SL Coupe, with its gullwing doors set to launch position. The iconic touch was the result of an engineering issue – normal doors wouldn't fit because of the space frame's tall side members. The workaround seems to have been successful. What didn't work as well was that the car had fixed windows and lacked air conditioning, causing Americans to call it the "German sweat box"; although that hasn't seemed to affect its resale value.

A detour reveals some of the company's quirkier products over the years including a 1907 Milnes-Daimler Doppeldecker (double-decker), a bright red bus that plied the streets of London. Daimler provided the chassis for this early form of mass transportation. Among the celebrity vehicles on display is one of Pope John Paul II's bulletproof Popemobiles. The pontiff's familiar white seat in the rear was a dentist's chair, so used because it could be easily moved up and down.

As you wind your way down the ramps, make sure to take peek out a window of the museum overlooking their test track. A recent visit revealed a new model (covered with camouflage material to protect it from prying eyes and telephoto lenses) taking a few laps.

If all this salivating over vintage Mercedes-Benzes has you pining for one to drive on the nearby autobahn, you needn't follow Janis Joplin's example and pray for one. On the lower level of the museum, next to the gift shop, there's a showroom with classic cars for sale, some of which are even relatively affordable and will provide much more excitement than a souvenir t-shirt.

Mercedes-Benz Museum Mercedesstrasse 100, 70372 Stuttgart, Germany

www.mercedes-benz.com/en/mercedes-benz/classic/museum

The Porsche Museum: There is No Substitute

Porsche Museum Stuttgart

What holds as much steel as the Eiffel Tower and corrals the power of more than 20,000 horses? That would be the gleaming Porsche Museum in Stuttgart, Germany. The surplus of steel is due to the dramatic sharply cantilevered shape of the building while the horses, naturally, are due to the 80+ vehicles within its vast interior.

From humble beginnings, which included designing the original Volkswagen that we know as the Beetle, Ferdinand Porsche created an automotive empire whose success still reverberates today. The dynamic building is reflective of that legacy.

Outside the front entrance a 78-foot-tall sculpture featuring three Porsche 911s soars up into the sky, representing three generations of the company's iconic vehicle. The sculpture provides a hint of the excitement to come. Cars are rotated from a collection of more than 550 Porsches, so each visit yields new surprises. Each car also runs – they are periodically taken out as a "museum on wheels" and shown at events around the world. Near the ground floor entrance a window looks into a workshop, offering a glimpse of mechanics preparing the vehicles for classic car races.

Visitors begin at the top of the structure and wind their way down to the ground floor, strolling along a spiraled walkway as they admire the cars on view that are displayed like motoring equivalent of works-of-art. Unlike many auto museums, the cars are not set off behind barriers, so you can walk all around them and even peer inside. Although as our guide stated, "But be careful, if you touch it, you buy it." He was joking, I think.

Porsches today have a sleek reputation, but it wasn't always that way. The first vehicle you'll run into is an 1898 Egger-Lohner-Elektromobil Modell C-2 Phaeton; the old-fashioned buggy looks like it was purloined from the set of *Gunsmoke,* minus its horse. But this revolutionary vehicle is considered the first constructed by Ferdinand Porsche. He attached an electric motor to the chassis and used it as a vehicle to test his early theories of automotive design.

Another homage to the early days of the inventor is a 1912 Austro-Daimler Motorspritze. It's fire-engine red because, well, it is a fire engine. It reflects Porsche's fascination with the unique technical requirements for fighting fires. His pioneering breakthrough allowed a full crew, water pump, and hose to be carried on a motorized vehicle.

But enough of this lap around memory lane; you're here for the speed-mobiles and the Porsche Museum has those aplenty. The white car festooned with red spades that looks like it was pulled from a pack of playing cards is a 1922 Austro-Daimler ADS R Sascha. It represents the beginning of Porsche's racing tradition, winning at the Targa Florio road race in Sicily. In the two-passenger vehicle the mechanic's seat is staggered slightly behind the driver; it took so much power – with elbows flying – to steer the car that this configuration helped the driver avoid whacking the mechanic in the head.

The shiny aluminum 1939 Type 64 looks like a precursor to the Space Age. Even now its streamlined shape emerges like something from the future and can be considered the father of all Porsches.

In 1946, Porsche's son Ferdinand "Ferry" Porsche took over the company. He stated, "In the beginning I looked around but couldn't find the car I dreamt of, so I decided to build it myself."

The 1948 Porsche Type 356 Nr. 1 Roadster is the first production sports car built with the Porsche name on it. It's basically a souped-up Volkswagen with an engine tuned to a dizzying 35 horsepower. The ignition key is on the left to save precious seconds, allowing drivers to start it with two hands when charging out of the starting line at LeMans. A 1964 Porsche 911 2.0 coupe was one of the first 911s. Originally it was supposed to be called a 901 but Peugeot owned the rights to that name and wouldn't let Porsche use it. Elsewhere Porsches are lined up by the dozen in exhibits honoring models such as the 924, 928, and more.

Of course, this being the Porsche Museum, supercars are not left out. The 2014 Porsche 918 Spyder cost close to a million dollars. For that you get an 887-horsepower hybrid engine and bragging rights. Nearby, a more sedate Porsche's top speed is only 12 miles per hour. That's because it's a tractor. The 1959 Porsche Schlepper (gotta love that name) represents the company's brief foray into farming equipment.

For serious students of the marque, Ferdinand Porsche's original drawings are archived at the museum and are available to view with a prior appointment. Before you leave you can pick up an affordable Porsche in the gift shop where realistic scale models are for sale.

While you're in Stuttgart you can also visit the Mercedes-Benz Museum, which is only six miles away. The two museums offer a combined discount admission ticket.

Porsche Museum Porscheplatz 1, 70435 Stuttgart-Zuffenhausen, Germany

www.porsche.com/international/aboutporsche/porschemuseum

Flugzeuge, Züge und Autos:
(Planes, Trains and Automobiles)

Technik Museum Sinsheim Sinsheim & **Technik Museum Speyer** Speyer

When I spoke at the World Forum for Motor Museums in Germany I had the opportunity to visit two of the most outstanding transportation museums in the world: the Technik Museum Sinsheim and the Technik Museum Speyer.

It's not every museum that boasts an actual SST perched on its roof. So, it's a rather spectacular sight to show up in Sinsheim and see not one, but two, of these sleek aerodynamic airplanes angled for take off. The museum, along with its sister property, the Technik Museum Speyer, offers an astonishing array of transportation including not just planes, trains, and automobiles, but also motorcycles, boats, fire trucks, armored military vehicles, a Russian space shuttle, submarines, tractors, trucks, bulldozers, a carousel, and more.

A visitor could easily spend several days at these attractions located about an hour south of Frankfurt. As a bonus, they are just 25 miles apart from one another, with the legendary autobahn in between them. Get a good rental car for the drive; even at 100 mph you'll easily be passed by the usual passel of luxury German automobiles.

The museums are the brainchild of the father-son team of Eberhard and Hermann Layher. The voluble Hermann runs the museums these days and puts his natural showman skills to good use. When a supersonic Russian Tupolev 144 SST became available, he figured it would be nice touch for the museum, so he bought it and had it hoisted onto the roof, inspired, he says, by seeing model airplanes displayed on pylons in a toy store. But it's true what they say about buying large aircraft, it's hard to stop at just one. Layher followed up this purchase with an Air France Concorde, a Lufthansa 747, several propeller planes, and the pièce de résistance, a Russian Buran space shuttle. What makes the displays even more special; visitors can climb inside each of the aircraft.

The two collections feature a wildly eclectic mix of automobiles. At Sinsheim, one of the standouts is the legendary Blue Flame. In 1970 Gary Gabelich set a land speed record in it on the Bonneville Salt Flats. The rest of the museum features more than 300 cars in several buildings representing a wide span of automotive history. One of the oldest cars is an American-built 1904 Columbia electric car once owned by the Rockefeller family.

A lineup of Opels includes a 1912 Opel 24/50 that spent much of its life in Australia; the dry climate contributing to its mostly original appearance. A precursor to the Volkswagen in the economy car category is a 1926 Hanomag, nicknamed the "Kommisbrot," (army bread), due to its loaf-like shape. One of the cost saving measures is apparent at first glance: it only has one headlight – but at least it's centered.

Naturally Mercedes-Benz models are in abundance with well over two dozen on display. Tastes run from classy, a 1934 500K, to sporty, three Mercedes 300 SLs, two of which are 1955 gullwings.

Some prime samples from the vintage American sector include a 1937 Cord 812; 1954, 1955 and 1956 Corvettes; 1958 Chevy Impala convertible; and a snow-white 1961 Chrysler 300G convertible showing off its muscle.

Aircraft geeks should be prepared to do some climbing to get into the two SSTs perched high above the auto barn. Pitched at takeoff angle, striding up the aisles will satisfy your fitness requirement for the day. Several other '50s and '60s-era passenger aircraft are also poised in mid-air for your visit.

Ah, but what about trains? The museum has that covered with a Maffei 1919 steam locomotive that is hooked up to an electric motor so visitors can press a button to watch the wheels go round and round. The engine is so massive that it was driven to the museum site on specially built tracks; the building was constructed around it.

The car collection at the Technik Museum Speyer is also outstanding. Yes, there's a Mercedes gullwing on display, but what really turns heads is an elegant car that tried to compete with it, a 1957 BMW 503 Cabriolet. Another highlight is a rare 1930 Maybach Zeppelin that was both the height of luxury and quality in its day. A 1963 Auto Union 1000 SP can easily be mistaken for a '55 Thunderbird and was in fact the German auto industry's answer to that American classic.

Naturally there is a 747 perched several stories overhead that you can climb up and into – including a chance to channel your inner daredevil and take a walk out on the wing. The plane is banked, giving you a slight funhouse experience navigating angled floors as you explore inside the massive bird. You can even crawl down into the baggage hold to see the mystery place where your luggage hopefully ends up during a flight.

In addition to the automotive and aviation collection, the museum devotes a separate hall to the largest exhibition in Europe of space flight, the highlight of which is the Soviet space shuttle; it's the only space shuttle located outside of the United States or Russia that can be found in a museum. There's also a permanent exhibition titled "Apollo and Beyond" that highlights the American and Soviet space programs.

After peeking inside the cargo bay of the space shuttle, I was descending the gangway when I heard an Aussie say, in that typical Down Under manner, as he gazed up at the vast building, "That's impressive. Not only do they have a space shuttle, but they have a shed to put the bloody thing in." That "shed" is larger than an airplane hangar and sums up these two museums perfectly: big, bold, and impressive.

Technik Museum Sinsheim Museumsplatz D-74889 Sinsheim, Germany
   sinsheim.technik-museum.de/en

Technik Museum Speyer Am Technik Museum 1, D-67346 Speyer, Germany
   speyer.technik-museum.de/en

Note: The museum owns the Hotel Sinsheim, which is adjacent to the Technik Museum Sinsheim. www.hotel-sinsheim.de/en

ACHTUNG, TRABI:
SALUTING THE LITTLE CAR IN BERLIN

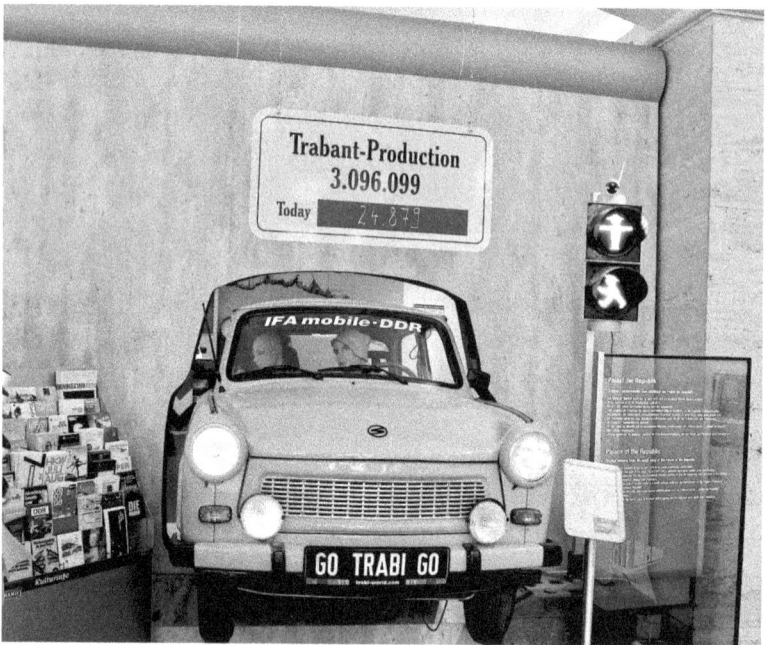

TRABI MUSEUM Berlin

When the Berlin Wall fell in 1989 it marked the impending death knell of a ubiquitous East German automobile – the diminutive Trabant – which rolled off assembly lines from 1957 through 1991. The name itself means "satellite" in German, inspired by the Soviet Union's Sputnik, which was launched the same year as the car.

While it has made several "worst car lists," the fact remains that, for a generation of East Germans, it was the go-to vehicle for those living behind the Iron Curtain and was cleverly adapted to many uses. The joke was that the car was so popular that people were willing to wait a decade for one; perhaps the long wait was why the average lifespan of a Trabant was 28 years. (Ironically, that's the same number of years that the Berlin Wall lasted.)

The history of the Trabant is told in all its dubious glory at the Trabi Museum in Berlin. Located just a block from popular tourist attraction Checkpoint Charlie, the museum continues the Cold War vibe as it greets visitors in the lobby with a 1963 Trabant 601 limousine that, in a moment of triumph, smashes through a replica of the Berlin Wall. A sign overhead states Trabant Production 3,096,099. Trabants were produced by VEB Sachsenring Automobilewerke Zwickau at their plant in Zwickau, formerly the pre-war home of Auto Union.

The Trabant wasn't created in a vacuum, and the museum starts out with a nod to its influences. A DKW F2, produced from 1932 through 1935, is presented as the 'grandfather' of the Trabant; its air-cooled two-stroke engine inspired the latter car's much maligned power base. It sits beside a flashy orange AWZ P70 Coupe – produced from 1957 through 1959 – that helped pioneer the use of Duroplast, an auto body material that was later used for Trabants. The material was fabricated from recycled cotton imported from the Soviet Union that was then blended with phenol resins.

The first Trabants were produced in 1957. Known as the P50, or 500, they featured a 500cc engine. The two-tone green-and-cream model on display is outfitted for a road trip with a rooftop luggage holder. Next to it is its successor, the Trabant 600. Produced for only a few years, the two-stroke engine saw an increase in horsepower from 20 to 23.

Visitors are encouraged to accordion themselves into an original P601 model (produced from 1963 through 1990) to get a feel for the austere interior. Older visitors share a knowing nostalgic look with each other as they awkwardly extract themselves from the tight confines of the vehicle.

The versatility of the little car that could is on view with a wide variety of uses. A 1987 Trabant 601 was 1 of 5 outfitted as a police test vehicle. The experiment didn't pan out (perhaps the 23-hp engine had something to do with it) and law enforcement continued driving Skodas and Wartburgs.

One area where the car was put to productive use was as a camper van. In the 1970s Gerhard Muller developed the Trabant car roof tent that slept two, providing a fleeting moment of freedom in the outdoors for people who were heavily surveilled at home by their government. In typical East German style, there was a waiting period of three years for this popular accessory.

As evidenced by a multitude of YouTube videos, the Trabant has also become an unexpectedly popular rally racing car. (Although it does seem prone to rollover.) Driven by Steffen Grossmann, the Trabant 601 here achieved a top speed of 195km/hour on its modified two-stroke 600cc engine pushing out 80hp.

Finally, after decades of relative sameness, in November 1988 the Trabant 1.1 was released. The model on display here is the first one assembled and sports the zippy new four-stroke engine with 40 hp that was licensed from Volkswagen. Alas, the dream of a new-and-improved Trabant was not to be. Within a year global events superseded the car as the Berlin Wall fell and the Trabant, like the wall itself, was tossed into the rubbish bin of history.

However, the car turned out to be more enduring than originally envisaged. After their demise, millions of Trabants were cluttering the driveways of a now-united Germany. In a full-circle solution, the cars were dismantled at the plant in Zwickau where they were originally produced and, after removing the metal for salvage, Duroplast bodies were shredded and recycled into bricks for pavement construction.

Thus, the car that was initially made from recycled materials still lives on as the oft maligned, yet curiously beloved little Trabi, proves that it is a true survivor.

Trabi Museum Zimmerstraße 14-15, 10969 Berlin, Germany
www.Trabi-Museum.com

GREECE

Axle Greece:
Motoring Heritage in Athens

HELLENIC MOTOR MUSEUM Athens

The city of Athens is renowned for attractions that are several millennia old. Yet the comparatively recent antiquities at the Hellenic Motor Museum consistently place the site on Trip Advisor's list of the city's top ten museums. Opened in 2011, the museum was founded by real estate developer (and competitive racer) Theodore Charagionis and his wife Joanna.

Located in an iconic helix-shaped building, the display ambles over three stories; at any one time, more than 100 cars are on display from a collection three times that size. Vehicles are broken out by era: Veteran, Vintage, Post Vintage, Classic, Post Classic, and

Modern – ranging from a 1906 Ford Model N two-seater runabout to a 1980 Ferrari GTSi. All the cars are kept in running condition.

Placards (in Greek and English) outline each car's engine type, output, top speed, and number produced. Most also list how they were acquired, with auctions in the UK a predominant method.

Highlights of the Vintage era include a 1921 Alvis 12/60 Beetleback roadster (a week after it was acquired in 1990, Charagionis won a 400km regularity rally in it), a 1926 Avion Viosin C4 Roadster, and a 1930 Bugatti Type 44 Drophead Coupe producing 80bhp. A 1927 Lincoln Sport Roadster Model L151 was discovered in the mid-1970s half buried in the mud of the Ilissos River, resulting in a thorough restoration to its current sparkling condition.

Post Vintage cars include a 1934 Bugatti Type 57 Ventoux (one of 630 produced), a 1937 Chrysler set up in police livery for a Captain America movie, and a 1939 Rolls-Royce Wraith Sports Sedan whose first owner was actor Laurence Olivier.

In the Classics area two barn-find 1950 Bristol 401 Saloons sitting side-by-side tell a tale of contrasts. One is still in its rough as-found condition, while the other – which was discovered in even worse condition – has been pristinely restored. If the double kidney grille looks familiar it's because it's based on designs Bristol acquired from BMW after the war. Another '50s beauty comes courtesy of a British 1955 Daimler Conquest Roadster. A pair of Lagondas includes a 1951 2.6-liter saloon and a 1955 MkII drophead coupe. A 1960 Daimler SP 250 Dart rounds out the section.

A 1962 Facel Vega Facellia F2B, 1966 Maserati Mistral Coupe, and a 1968 Jensen Interceptor FF1 represent swinging '60s style. The following decade is embodied by fine Italian hardware, including a 1972 Alfa Romeo Montreal, 1974 Iso Rivolta Lele, and a 1974 Ferrari 365 GT4 Berlinetta Boxer.

The "Made by Hellas" area is devoted to automobiles with Greek connections: the most popular of which is the output of Sir Alec Issigonis. The British designer of Greek descent was instrumental in the look of the original Mini and the Morris Minor. Enfield Automotive, funded by Greek shipping magnate Giannis

Goulandris, developed the 1974 Enfield E8000 ECC (Electric City Car) to create a non-gas-powered vehicle for urban use. The diminutive profile of the car was the shape of things to come.

A pale turquoise 1977 MEBEA Robin appears ready to tumble over. Produced in Greece under license from the UK-based Reliant Motor Company, the three-wheeler automobile sports a curvy fiberglass body.

The "Transparency" display is a fascinating exhibit. Five vehicles – including a 1964 Lancia Flavia convertible and a 1974 Lotus Europa Twin Cam Special – are essentially deconstructed, in some cases with their bodies partially lifted off the chassis, so visitors can literally see what's under the hood and more. According to guide Miltos Petronis, "People are drawn to the exposed cars to see what makes them go."

Hellenic Motor Museum Ioulianou 33-35, Athens, Greece
www.HellenicMotorMuseum.gr/en

ITALY

Alfa Romeo:
Heritage, Beauty, and Speed

Alfa Romeo Historical Museum Arese

I must admit, I approached the Museo Storico Alfa Romeo (Alfa Romeo Historical Museum) in Arese, Italy with a sense of bittersweet nostalgia. Years ago, my wife Larissa and I owned a 1988 Spider Quadrifoglio, naturally in "Alfa Red." With its sleek lines, it looked like it would get a speeding ticket while standing still. Ironically, the 115-horsepower engine was more suited to ambling along country lanes, unlikely to outpace a bog-standard Ford or Vauxhall from a stoplight.

But "Alfie" was a still a beauty, and soon we were spending many a weekend attending Alfa club road rallies, our shiny red convertible dappled by shade on those country lanes. Alas, the honeymoon was not to last. I'll spare you all the gritty details but, despite those Italian good looks, our Alfie was not exactly a reliable car and after a few years we finally sold it. But the warm memory lived on; it's still the car we've driven where the most people would pull up alongside and give us a hearty thumbs-up.

Which is why we were in northern Italy on a crisp autumn day to learn all about the history of Alfa Romeo style and hoping to discover a bit more about the substance behind this stylish marque.

The 200-car collection sprawling over six stories is laid out in three sections, focusing on heritage, beauty, and speed. The museum begins with its A.L.F.A. (Anonima Lombarda Fabbrica Automobili) collection before it merged during World War I with Nicola Romeo & Company to create the legendary marque we know today: Alfa Romeo.

Heritage

Visitors begin their visit with a stroll through a timeline of Alfa vehicles starting with a 1910 A.L.F.A 24 hp and a 1911 A.L.F.A 15 hp Corsa with a sporty torpedo body from the very early years. Next to them, a 1925 RL Super Sport adorned in a brushed aluminum body, formerly owned by an Indian Maharaja, represents the second generation of high-performance Alfas.

The post-war gallery features smaller, more elegant fare including a 1950 1900 (it was introduced at that year's Paris Auto Show), 1954 1900 Super Sport and a 1955 Giulietta. A section on Alfas in film pays homage to famous movie cars, including the 1966 1600 Spider "Duetto" roadster driven by Dustin Hoffman in The Graduate – which would serve as the inspiration for this author's purchase, along with many others, years later.

The 1970s are represented by the bright orange Montreal 200 hp 2+2 (barely) coupé, which debuted as a concept car at Expo 67 in Montreal and then hit the road in numbers in 1970.

Beauty

Head to the lower level for "The Masters of Style" gallery. Here, eight cars that have broken the automotive design mold showcase the breadth of Alfa Romeo. The first vehicle, a 1913 Castagna Aerodinamica built on an A.L.F.A. 40-60 HP chassis, with its shimmery Zeppelin shape, appears to be purloined from a Jules Verne novel. Its porthole windows really do make it look ready to venture 20,000 leagues under the sea.

Next to it is another aeronautically inspired vehicle, the 1952 Alfa Romeo 1900 C52 Disco Volante (Flying Saucer). Built with Milan-based coachbuilder Touring as a potential race car, only five were produced. Similar streamlined styling was seen later on Jaguar's legendary D-Type.

According to Alfa, with the advent of the lime-green mid-engine 1969 Carabo "the car was no longer a bundle of sinuous muscles but a sharp blade." True enough, the hood on the pioneering supercar looks sharp enough to slice open a wheel of Cheddar.

Speed

Not surprisingly, the Speed section is the most exciting. Shiny red champion cars are lined up against walls that are covered floor to ceiling with movies highlighting Alfa Romeo's racing heritage. An immersive sound and light show drops visitors into the center of the racetrack as Alfas capture the checkered flag again and again. Any marque with a young Enzo Ferrari's involvement – he started as a driver there in 1920 – certainly can claim bragging rights when it comes to racing heritage.

The 1923 Alfa Romeo RL, piloted by Ugo Sivocci, won the 1923 Targa Florio. It was the first Alfa adorned with the lucky charm of a green cloverleaf on a white background that would become symbolic of Alfa Romeo excellence. Vittorio Jano designed the 1925 Alfa Romeo GP Tipo P2 that won the Italian and European Grand Prix races that year. It featured Alfa's straight 8-cylinder supercharged engine with two carburetors placed after the compressor.

In 1929 Enzo Ferrari set up Scuderia Ferrari (Ferrari Stable) as Alfa's racing arm. His iconic prancing horse symbol first appeared on Alfa Romeo race cars like the shark-finned 1935 Bimotore, which featured dual supercharged 2.9-liter eight-cylinder motors both fore and aft. They were connected by two driveshafts to a single gearbox to achieve 540 combined horsepower and a top speed of 226 mph. The dual-engine configuration placed the fuel tanks on the side so, not surprisingly, with the increased horsepower, the car was difficult to handle on the curve.

Alfa's post-war racing years were led by the 158/159 Alfetta line. Although designed before the war, the cars dominated the newly inaugurated Formula 1 World Championship races starting in 1950. A 1951 GP Tipo 159 Alfetta chassis is displayed without its hood to reveal the powerful 425 hp vertical straight-eight engine with one triple-choke carburetor and dual two-stage superchargers in series.

Later successes on view include the 1968 Tipo 33/2 Daytona, 1975 Tipo 33 TT12 – a tubular chassis and 12-cylinder engine led it to 7 victories in 8 tries – and a 1977 Tipo 33 SC 12 Turbo which achieved 8 wins in 8 races. The hand-built, mid-engine 1967 33 Stradale prototype was another pioneering supercar that could reach 162 mph.

In addition to the vehicles, engines are displayed on pedestals throughout the museum along with a wall of model cars.

After seeing all the heritage, beauty, and speed of Alfa Romeo arrayed in one place, I left with a new appreciation for the vaunted marque. Perhaps there's another one in my future after all. This is one of the few motoring museums that has a new car showroom attached so it is tempting to ditch the rental car and hit the autostrada in search of another thumbs-up.

Alfa Romeo Historical Museum Viale Alfa Romeo, 20020 Arese, Italy
www.MuseoAlfaRomeo.com/en-us

Grand Torino!
Visiting Italy's Motor City

Fiat Museum (Centro Storico Fiat) Torino

With an automotive manufacturing heritage dating to 1895, Torino, Italy (known in English as Turin), can rightly claim to be the Detroit of Italy. Today it is the home of major operations for Stellantis (Fiat Chrysler) and General Motors' international powertrain development business, but classic car buffs have plenty to explore here. Two world-class car museums, plus a former rooftop test track that achieved cinematic fame, are all within walking distance of one another making Torino a worthwhile destination.

Driven by Passion

The Fiat Museum (Centro Storico Fiat) is housed in a circa 1907 Art Nouveau former Fiat manufacturing facility. After Fiat co-founder Giovanni Agnelli visited a Ford factory in 1912, he modernized the building and introduced an assembly line here. The spacious museum features nearly three-dozen vehicles, engines and scale models spread out over two levels against a backdrop of oversized vintage Fiat marketing posters. A large skylight illuminates the premises with natural daylight.

One of the most iconic racing cars here is the 1908 Fiat SB4. Nicknamed "Mefistofele," or the Devil's Machine, it was fitted with a 325-horsepower Fiat aircraft straight-six engine by Sir Ernest Eldridge; in 1924 he set a World Land Speed Record on a closed public road of 234.98 km/hour. Parked nearby is the 1933 503 S Balilla Mille Miglia that was known as the "Queen of the 1100 cc class" due to its successes in the Mille Miglia, Traga Florio, and Coppa d'Oro races.

Perhaps the most elegant car in the museum is the two-toned black-and-gray 1929 Fiat 525 SS; only a few dozen were built of the car that Automobile Quarterly called "one of the five most beautiful models of all time."

The 1936 Fiat 500 Topolino (the Italian name for Mickey Mouse) is from the first year of this iconic vehicle, which was the world's smallest mass-produced car. The 569cc engine was cantilevered over the front axle for the "baby" Fiat.

A rare vehicle is the one-of-a-kind prototype for the 1940 Fiat 700; presented to Mussolini in May 1939, the bridge between the Fiat 500 Topolino and Fiat 1100 never entered production due to the war.

Looking back, the introduction in 1956 of the jellybean-shaped multi-purpose Fiat 600 Multipla, with its three rows of seating, can be considered the precursor of the minivan. According to the museum, "Its versatility was far ahead of its time. Too far ahead," and sales were poor. However, by 1964 the model on display sported a larger 767 cc engine – that helped it become a workhorse of the Italian taxi industry – while its signature styling became a symbol of the country's post-war economic boom.

Despite its sporty reputation, Fiat also made a few workhorses. One of them is the 1919 Fiat 702 tractor that was adaptable to many situations; special wheels fit on railroad tracks to tow light trains and it could also be set up as a generator.

The second level of the museum, a gallery that rings the huge skylight, is devoted to Fiat's other areas of manufacturing expertise, including aircraft and ship engines. Somehow, they squeezed in a Fiat G 91 R/1 fighter/photo reconnaissance jet used by NATO forces. Nearby, a display of more than two dozen scale model airplanes that appear poised for takeoff line a 30-foot-long mirrored shelf, highlighting the breadth of Fiat's offerings in aviation. The gallery also features a display of vintage marketing Fiat marketing materials, including original vintage advertising posters and brochures.

The Italian Job

Fiat soon grew out of the factory that now houses its museum and in 1923 built a massive new facility in the nearby Lingotto manufacturing district; it's so large that a test track was put on the roof. One of the most memorable chase scenes from the 1969 Michael Caine movie *The Italian Job* was filmed on the rooftop track. Though the factory is now closed, the structure has survived. It was redeveloped into a mixed-use facility, housing offices of Fiat Chrysler Automobiles, a shopping mall and the DoubleTree by Hilton Turin Lingotto. Keeping with the automotive theme, the hotel's corridors are lined with blueprints and photos of the original factory.

It's worth booking a room at the hotel; guests are given access to the rooftop test track which is, unbelievably, still intact with its steeply banked curves. The building's original ramps that spiral upwards through what is now the mall are blocked to prevent someone trying to recreate the movie's chase scene. For now, you can satisfy yourself with walking along the track while gazing out onto the rooftops of Torino. Perched above the track is the Pinacoteca Agnelli, a jewel-box museum containing the art collection of former Fiat chairman Giovanni "Gianni" Agnelli and his wife Marella, which is also free to DoubleTree hotel guests.

The original scene from the movie is available on YouTube.

Fiat Museum Via Gabriele Chiabrera, 20, 10126 Torino, Italy
www.fcaheritage.com/en-uk/heritage/places/centro-storico-fiat

Note: As of my visit, admission to the museum was free, but it was only open on Sundays.

NATIONAL AUTOMOBILE MUSEUM (Museo Nazionale dell' Automobile) Torino

With an automotive manufacturing heritage dating to 1895, Torino, Italy (known in English as Turin), can rightly claim to be the Detroit of Italy.

The vast National Automobile Museum (Museo Nazionale dell'Automobile) opened in 1960, founded by automotive enthusiast and journalist Carlo Biscaretti di Ruffia, who unfortunately died the year before its opening. After undergoing a large-scale transformation in 2011 and 2014, the sleek modern building featuring 200 vehicles spanning 80 marques reflects its Italian heritage by offering a highly stylized way to view the history of the automotive industry, both from Italy and around the world. The museum's mission is ambitious: to tell the history of the motoring industry through those 200 vehicles.

While the museum is like other collections in that there are many cars on display, there are also clever interactive exhibits that highlight the driving experience and Turin's role in it. With more than two-dozen galleries inside the museum, visitors can easily spend a day or two here.

Simple cars from the early days of Italian motoring include a 1908 FIAL (not Fiat) Legnano; the "Duc" style body resembled a horse-drawn carriage with only two seats and a folding top to protect passengers. The maker was active in Lombardy from 1906 through 1909.

An exhibited titled "The Italian Revolution" celebrates the post-World War II marriage of industry and art in the revival of the Italian automobile industry. A flame-red 1948 Cisitalia 202, in all its supple glory, is surrounded by larger-than-life schematic drawings. The high cost of its Pinan Farina coach-built body precluded wide production. Its cousin, a 1946 Cisitalia 202 GT, was the first car acquired by the Museum of Modern Art in New York where it is referred to as "rolling sculpture."

Across from the Cisitalia sits a 1954 Fiat Turbina, whose unexpected Batmobile-style tailfins rival those on a '59 Caddy. Almost a decade before Chrysler's famous turbine car, the Fiat's propulsion was provided by a two-stage turbine engine that reached 22,000 RPM to provide 300 hp capable of reaching 150 mph. The placard realistically states: "A sophisticated, intriguing, aerodynamic prototype – Without a future."

Another nod to new technology is the West German 1966 NSU Ro 80 whose Wankel engine is described as "Quiet, Light, and Fast. But as for its fuel consumption . . . it will remain a passing fad."

Not all new technology was a failure. In the *Mechanical Symphony* gallery, the chassis of a 1924 Lancia Lambda is displayed at eye-level, nearly perpendicular to the ground to showcase its revolutionary unibody construction. The chassis of a 1928 Alfa Romeo 6C 1500 Mille Miglia Speciale is similarly exposed.

Since the museum emphasizes motion, the display of a dozen wheels, ranging from a medieval wooden cart wheel through a 1910 wooden wheel with a studless Michelin tire up to a modern steel wheel, are all spinning. Interactivity is present throughout the museum. In one area, visitors sit in a chair and slide a large metal drum-like structure around their head. Inside, a video screen offers a wide selection of vintage television car ads from around the world; some of the Japanese ads are the most entertaining.

Unusual cars I've not seen elsewhere include a VW Beetle competitor – the 1958 Lloyd Alexander TS, built by the Borgward Group, was powered (just barely) by an air-cooled two-cylinder engine that put out 29 hp – and a diminutive 1959 Autobianchi Bianchina that looks like it could fit in one's pocket.

One of the most interesting rooms I've come across in a car museum is the cleverly named *Autorino* gallery that focuses on Turin's role as Italy's Motor City. Here, more than seventy auto manufacturers – including Fiat in 1899 – and eighty coachbuilders were once active. A tribute to this heritage is splayed out beneath visitors, who stroll atop a fifty-by-fifty-foot backlit photo map of the city. Color-coded markers show where each of the city's auto manufacturers were located and give the dates of their existence. Like a life-sized version of Google Maps, it's fascinating to navigate the streets and place storied names in context.

Other galleries include: *David and Goliath*, comparing tailfin era American cars with European microcars of the same time period; *Goodbye Lenin*, which features Iron Curtain cars like the Soviet-built 1957 GAZ M-20 Pobeda and the ubiquitous East German 1987 Trabant 601, (which looks like it's from a prior decade because the design actually was); and *Luxury Motor Car*, featuring early posh rides like a 1909 Itala 35/45 HP, 1909 Isotta Fraschini AN 20/30 HP, and a 1913 Delage AB-8.

Rather than just reveling in the past, the future of automotive design is on display in a ground floor gallery where prototypes built by students in the Transportation Design division of Turin's Istituto Europeo di Design (European Design Institute) are presented.

Spoiler alert: Classic car fans may not be enamored of these sinewy, wind tunnel designed forms, but they still look pretty cool.

This museum is large enough that you could easily spend a day here and not see everything, so plan accordingly.

National Automobile Museum (Museo Nazionale dell'Automobile)
Corso Unità d'Italia 40, 10126 Torino, Italy
www.MuseoAuto.com/en

Molto Veloce in Italy's Motor Valley

Museo Enzo Ferrari/Museo Ferrari/Museo Lamborghini/ Collezione Umberto Panini Motor Museum Modena

With its soaring 12th-century cathedral spire and cobblestoned streets, the ancient city of Modena hardly looks like an industrial powerhouse, but it's the center of the Motor Valley where Ferrari, Lamborghini, and Maserati automobiles, along with Ducati motorcycles, are built. Modena is the birthplace of Enzo Ferrari, whose bright red, road-hugging vehicles seem synonymous with the word "racecar." Located in the Emilia-Romagna region 250 miles north of Rome, visitors can tour factories and museums related to these legendary marques.

Start your Motor Valley tour at the **Museo Enzo Ferrari** in Modena. You'll walk in the legendary carmaker's footsteps at his original workshop and home (in true "live fast" style, Ferrari inherited the house at age 20, but sold it soon afterward to buy a sports car) while getting up close to the first road Ferrari ever built, a 1947 Ferrari 125 S, and more than 30 high-performance engines.

Adjacent to the workshop a newer building's striking yellow roof curves skyward, mimicking the hood of a 1950s racing Ferrari. Inside, over 20 Ferraris are displayed under glittery lights as if they were jewels in a crown, although these Italian creations are more expensive than most diamonds.

Ferraris here include a 1948 Ferrari Aerlux 2+2 outfitted with an Aerlux sunroof; a 1964 Ferrari 500 Superfast whose V12 reached 400 hp; and a 2007 Ferrari Scaglietti 60.

Other marques include a 1903 De Dion Bouton like the one that Enzo Ferrari's father owned; a 1921 Alfa Romeo G1; and a 1962 Maserati Sebring. Racing cars vary but include a 1996 F310 driven by Michael Schumacher to victory in the 1996 Spanish Grand Prix.

The music of another local legend, opera star Luciano Pavarotti, soars over the proceedings creating a sense of autos as art and gets you in the mood for the next stop of the day.

www.MuseoModena.Ferrari.com

Ferrari moved production to nearby Maranello in the 1940s. There, the **Museo Ferrari** focuses more on performance with a dose of heritage thrown in. The visitor's path winds its way through Ferrari Formula 1 race cars up to the "One-Off" gallery that includes Eric Clapton's SP12EC. Make sure to enjoy the museum; the only way to see where the Ferraris are actually built is to buy one.

www.MuseoMaranello.Ferrari.com

For a chance to step out onto a supercar factory floor head 12 miles east of Modena to the country village of Sant' Agata for the **Museo Lamborghini**. Despite the village's quaint confines, you might find yourself getting dusted by a brand-new Lamborghini on your way there since the company uses public roads as their test track. In the factory you'll tour the assembly line where all Lamborghinis are handcrafted. It takes three days to make each car and they churn out only ten Aventadors and Huracáns daily. You'll learn fun facts like how seven pristine cattle hides are used to meticulously outfit the interior of each luxe vehicle.

The museum adjacent to the workshop displays about two dozen autos, including one for a very lucky police department: the 2004 Gallardo-Polizia Stradale squad car was one of only two built and cranked up to 500 horsepower.

www.lamborghini.com/en/museum

For a taste of vintage autos start out at the free **Collezione Umberto Panini Motor Museum** located on the southern outskirts of Modena. The first thing that strikes the eye upon approaching the entrance is an antique Lamborghini tractor sitting out front, a reminder of the prestigious automaker's humble roots as a manufacturer of farm equipment.

The museum itself focuses on the Maserati brand from 1914 until present times. (It's a good thing too. Even though Maserati's trident logo towers over their headquarters in Modena, they do not offer factory tours or a museum of their own.) In the Panini Museum you'll find over 100 vehicles including 40 cars and 60 motorcycles. The Maserati 420M Eldorado was built for Stirling Moss to race in the 1958 "500 Miles of Monza." Eldorado was an ice cream maker, and the car represents a major step in outside companies sponsoring Italian auto racing.

www.PaniniMotorMuseum.it

After spending several days touring primo cars motor back to Modena and reward yourself with a fine Italian meal in the town that invented tortellini pasta and the eponymous balsamic vinegar di Modena. Mangia!

GETTING ARRESTED IN STYLE

STATE POLICE CAR MUSEUM (Museo delle Auto della Polizia di Stato) Rome

The Museo delle Auto della Polizia di Stato in Rome is a bit like an undercover operative. The online presence is minimal, and its location, in an off-the-beaten-track neighborhood well south of Rome's main tourist attractions, is understated. But for the intrepid explorer, it yields a unique museum devoted solely to police vehicles. From little 1950s-era Fiats to a supercar Lamborghini, the evolution of Italian police cars has kept pace with the criminals they are meant to capture.

The vehicles of State Police in Italy are distinguished by livery that is painted in "Police Medium Blue" with a white stripe. The blue is similar to that worn by the Italian national soccer team.

The 70-vehicle display focuses on the post-World War II era and is broken up into separate rows by decade. To put the eras in context, each row is decorated with posters of relevant events in world and Italian history that were taking place when the cars were plying the streets of Italy. The vehicle information placards are all in Italian, but with the rudimentary Italian I derived from my immigrant grandparents I could decipher most of them.

The 1952 Fiat C Topolino lives up to (or perhaps "down") to its nickname, which in Italian means "Little Mouse," with its 567 cc, 16.5 hp motor reluctantly pushing it to 60 mph. Looking a little more fearsome, the 1951 Fiat 1100 EL four-door sedan was known as the "Muzzle" due its large full-height front grille. The 1089 cc engine delivered 35 horsepower, more than double that of the Topolino. A pair of Alfa Romeos – a 1961 2000 Sprint and 1964 2600 Sprint – show that crime fighting can by stylish too.

The 1969 Fiat AR/55 Campagnola (Country Reconnaissance Vehicle) with its green paint and jeep-like lines looks it could have stepped out of a World War II-era U.S. Army film. In fact, it was the result of a post-war contest by the Italian government for car manufacturers to create something akin to the Willys jeep. Due to its lower price, the Fiat won out over Alfa Romeo's entry in the contest. Its ruggedness led to the model's original advertising jingle in 1951: "the go-anywhere vehicle that doesn't need a road." It also features a large spotlight on the back for use during emergencies. A Fiat from the same year is a 1969 Fiat 124 Familiare station wagon.

The 1979 De Tomaso 892 Deauville appears to be a standard luxury four-door saloon. However, Alejandro De Tomaso was influenced by the design of the Jaguar XJ6. Even with its Maserati Quattroporte chassis and Jaguar-style independent suspension, only 244 were produced. What's not so apparent is that the model on display is a heavily armored version of the vehicle, one of only two built, used to transport high value individuals for the national government. Despite its extra weight, this beast could still reach speeds more than 120 mph. The remaining model was destined for the Belgian royal family.

The fastest car in the museum, the 2009 Lamborghini Gallardo Polizia, with a top speed over 180 MPH, was employed during emergencies for the rapid delivery of blood and organs; it also boasted an on-board defibrillator. In that regard, it was a real lifesaver.

One non-Italian car that made it to the national police force is the 2003 Subaru Legacy 2.5 Touring Wagon with all-wheel drive. Its 2500cc Boxer engine that reached 120 mph made it particularly suitable for law enforcement on the autostrade.

Two (and three) wheeled vehicles are also included – like the 1971 Moto Guzzi V7 motorcycle with sidecar. Only three were produced for use in motorcycle training and testing. The 1962 Motocarro da Montagna Moto Guzzi 3x3 was a three-wheeled treaded vehicle used for climbing steep mountain terrain. Dubbed the Mulo Meccanico (Mechanical Mule) it was prone to rollover and, unfortunately, not as stable as the donkeys it replaced.

Besides the full-size vehicles, there's also a collection of toy police cars on glass shelves. Assorted law enforcement paraphernalia include a Tag Heuer chronometer used to catch speeding drivers and uniform unit patches. On a side note, one of the most notable cars in the museum is a 1962 Ferrari 250 GTE. Unfortunately, it was not there during my visit.

Museo delle Auto della Polizia di Stato Via dell'Arcadia, 20, Rome, Italy
www.PoliziaDiStato.it/articolo/555

Note: Be aware that the hours listed on the web site are often more of a guideline; you may want to call ahead to confirm that they are open.

POLAND

Pole Position:
Polish Automotive Heritage in Krakow

Museum of Municipal Engineering Krakow

It's not often that I eagerly await the opening of something called the Museum of Municipal Engineering, but there I was in Krakow, Poland's second largest city and medieval capital, doing just that. What had attracted me was a blurb in a magazine referring to their Motorculture exhibit, which highlights the history of the Polish car industry from its early days, on through the years of producing Polish Fiats and various prototypes of mini-cars. It sounded intriguing.

The museum is housed in a series of turn-of-the-century brick structures that make up the former city tramway sheds, workshops, and power plant. Descriptions are in English as well as Polish. The focus is on post-war automotive production, with its emphasis on creating value with limited resources; many of the cars are so small they look like they could be picked up and taken away. In fact, after an accident or frequent breakdown, towing was often human powered.

A special car is a 1962 Syrena 101. The Syrena 101 was the only car developed by Polish engineers in the postwar era that made it into mass production. Belying its humble looks – and 1930s era design that was already obsolete – it was a high social status car, limited to labor leaders, scientists, and the like. Between 1957 and 1983, more than a half million of them were produced. The model on display is in a bright orange that is obviously not original, given away by the brushstrokes in the paint. As I was pondering it a 35-year-old local named Magdalena asked me to snap a photo of her and her 8-year-old son in front of the car.

It wasn't easy to get a car during the Communist era. She recalled, "It was the first car of my childhood. My parents didn't get it until I was five and it brings back such memories of when the only cars available were the Syrena, Warszawa, and the Polski Fiat. It was a brilliant design, it even had an ashtray in the rear seat. I also remember a hole in the floor to let out water." I asked if they came in the bright orange color, but she said all the ones she recalls were beige.

Magdalena's reference to the Polski Fiat brings up a lesser-known aspect of Poland's motoring history: its long track record as a manufacturing base for Fiat. Polski Fiats started production in the 1930s – represented here by a 1936 Polski Fiat 508 III Junak – but the war intervened and the relationship ended.

After a long hiatus, the partnership with Fiat began anew in 1967, resulting in the Polski Fiat 125p. It was a step up in the social ladder from the Syrena and was often reserved for party apparatchiks. Many were also exported to Egypt and Western Europe. Here a 1968 model in standard beige still holds true to its diminutive, elegant lines: looking almost like a mini-Lincoln. Almost.

In 1973 a smaller car, the Polski Fiat 126p (similar to a Fiat 500) emerged. This car still lives on in Polish folklore as the star of movies, cartoons, and even an art installation. Its wee stature led to many nicknames including the *maluch*, or toddler. Several of these pocket-sized autos are on display in the museum.

The 1959 Warszawa 200 four-door white sedan was the first model of the marque that private individuals could buy. Although with a price tag equivalent to eight years of an average worker's salary, few could afford to do so.

Possibly the most endearing econobox in the collection is a two-toned, blue-and-white 1959 Smyk microcar from the Szczecin Motorcycle Factory, with a single front door for entry: the entire front of the car, including the steering wheel, angles forward for ingress and egress. This is one of 20 prototypes: the car never made it to full production because, not surprisingly, it was underpowered and unsafe.

Another attempt at a Polish car was made in 1983. The metallic green 1983 FSM 106 Beskid prototype is one of eight that were produced. It offered an innovative monospace body, but the project was terminated due to lack of funds. Some claim the aerodynamic car was an inspiration for the later Renault Twingo, which very much resembles it.

Poland also has a long history of motorcycle production. A 1939 Podkowa 98 was produced based on a licensing agreement with Villiers. The advent of World War II limited production to 130 units. WFM-Warszawska Fabryka Motocykli (Warsaw Motorcycle Factory) motorcycles were the most popular bike during the 1950s, leading to early mass motorization of the country. The display example is a 1959 WFM.

A non-Polish car in the collection is a sky blue 1929 Durant Rugby Express L 16-seat bus. It was restored in 2010 and is fully operational to ply, for special occasions, the same Krakow streets on which it once carried passengers.

Don't be fooled by the understated name, the Museum of Municipal Engineering in Krakow is the perfect spot to learn more about automotive design behind the Iron Curtain and see many of these rare vehicles up close. Just don't be tempted to pick one up and walk away with it.

Museum of Municipal Engineering Świętego Wawrzyńca 15, 31-060 Kraków, Poland
www.mim.krakow.pl/en

ROMANIA

SERVING UP AUTOMOTIVE ACES IN ROMANIA

ȚIRIAC COLLECTION Otopeni

Anyone who watched professional tennis in the 1970s remembers a hulking, walrus-mustached Romanian player named Ion Țiriac. He often teamed up in doubles matches with his well-known countryman Ilie Nastase. Back then Romania was a little-known country firmly tucked away behind the Iron Curtain.

Flash forward to the new millennium; the Iron Curtain is just a memory and Romania is transforming into a leading country for high-tech industries. Țiriac's natural drive as an athlete enabled him to spot the new business opportunities that freedom offered on his way to becoming Romania's first billionaire and richest man. He has always been passionate about cars. His first purchase was a Skoda Octavia he bought in 1969, with earnings from winning multiple tennis tournaments. Fortunately for fans of classic and exotic cars, he continues that drive today in acquiring his wonderful collection of rare automobiles.

The Țiriac Collection is located on the outskirts of the capital of Bucharest, just across from the airport. In a little over a decade, the former tennis star has built up an impressive grouping of more than 400 vehicles, about 160 of which are on display at any one time. It contains an eclectic mix but focuses on high-end marques like Rolls-Royce, Mercedes-Benz, Aston Martin, Lamborghini, Ferrari, Porsche and surprisingly, a fair number of American cars.

They're displayed like rare baubles and kept in primo condition; in fact, it's also the only car museum I've visited where I had to slide plastic booties over my shoes to protect the cars from dirt. (Unfortunately, they were so slippery on the high-gloss floor that I almost crashed with my camera into a million-dollar vehicle.)

Rolls-Royces are most in abundance with 16 of them arrayed around the entrance; included are 6 Rolls-Royce Phantoms. The museum claims that it's the only gallery where you'll find all 6 Phantoms of the I-VI series. The 1960 Phantom V was owned by Elton John, who commissioned its flamboyant pink and white paint job with matching interior.

A V-12 couples with a hybrid motor on the sinewy 963 horsepower 2014 Ferrari LaFerrari. Only 499 were available to specially vetted customers. (Shark Tank star Robert Herjavec was also one of the lucky buyers.) A 500th was sold at a charity auction in December 2016 to benefit earthquake victims in Italy. At the time, the $7 million price was a record for a 21st-century automobile.

Another Italian masterpiece is a 2013 Ferrari F12 Berlinetta; the V-12 two-seater pushes out 730 horses. Despite all that power, one of the touted benefits of the car was increased luggage space. Who knew an exotic sports car could be so practical?

Perhaps a bit less practical is the 1991 Lamborghini Diablo with its rakish scissor doors; I couldn't help but think I'd keep hitting my head on them getting in and out of the vehicle. Naturally the three Italian supercars just mentioned were liveried in bright red.

Fans of Teutonic exotics are also in luck. A 2015 Porsche 918 Spyder mid-engine plug-in hybrid sports car is one of only 918 built. The V-8 and two electric motors combined crank out 887 horsepower reaching 210 mph. The top pipes are a sporty touch for the production vehicle.

The 2009 Mercedes SLR McLaren Stirling Moss Edition, that looks like it's ready to go airborne, is rare; indeed, it's one of a mere 75 that were built. It was only made available to prior SLR owners.

A bevy of British beauties that wouldn't look out of place in James Bond's garage include a royal blue 1981 Aston Martin V8 Vantage. (Widely considered to be the first British supercar when it premiered in 1977, these Aston Martins look strikingly like a classic Ford Mustang.) A 1960 Triumph TR3A and the occasional Jensen can be spotted in the collection, including a fiberglass-bodied, aluminum-door 1966 C-V8 Mk III Coupe. The winter-white 1960 Jaguar XK 150 Roadster is a rare example produced for the export market, which explains its left-hand drive for navigating on the "wrong" side of the road. (Well, at least from a British perspective.)

Although the collection focuses on European autos, more than a dozen American cars make the grade including: a 1995 Camaro Z28 police interceptor that's souped up with a 700-horsepower engine; and a fiery orange 1968 Dodge Charger R/T with only 296 miles on it. Because all the vehicle's batteries are plugged into a power source to keep them ready to start up, it was tempting to get behind the wheel and let 'er rip.

Taking a step decades back in time is a 1930 Duesenberg Model J Torpedo Berline Convertible that belonged to silver screen legend Tyrone Power. It's fitting in a collection with so many Rolls-Royces to see an American car that went toe-to-toe with them in the luxury market.

Țiriac Collection Calea Bucureștilor 289, Otopeni 075100, Romania www.TiriacCollection.ro/en

SLOVENIA

Iron Curtain Classics

Technical Museum of Slovenia Vrhnika

Would you buy a used car from Joseph Stalin? How about if it was given to you? That was the case for Josep Tito, the leader of Yugoslavia at the end of World War II. In 1945, when the Soviet leader wanted to thank Tito for his partisan fighting activities that helped lead to victory, he presented him with a 1937 Packard Twelve. Because Stalin had owned the car it was also, for security reasons, heavily armored. It's on display along with more than 55 cars and 50 motorcycles at the Technical Museum of Slovenia; one of the former Yugoslav republics that is now an independent country. The museum is only a half-hour drive southwest from the capital of Ljubljana.

The cars that were used by President Tito are set up in a barn and are part of a larger car exhibit located at a 16th-century Carthusian monastery that houses the collection. Also located on the ambling grounds are museums devoted to forestry, hunting, fishing, and industrial trades. But the largest amount of space is devoted to transportation.

The hands-on displays range from wall-mounted wooden steering wheels, that are turned to reveal tidbits of automotive history, to touch screens next to the cars for the visitor to learn more information about them.

It appears that Tito had a penchant for American metal. Other cars he used are a 1936 Cadillac V-12, 1942 Cadillac Series 67, and a 1954 Cadillac Eldorado, with its rather pronounced Dagmar bumpers protruding from the front grille. Tito didn't seem too particular about marques; he was also squired around in a 1965 Lincoln Continental convertible.

One hefty car that could be mistaken for an army tank is a 1954 Soviet ZIS-115, a gift from Stalin's successor, Nikita Khrushchev. With windows that are 3 inches thick and raised and lowered via a hydraulic system, it's the armored version of the ZIS-110. It stands out from Tito's American cars by sporting a hood ornament that is comprised of a red Soviet banner emblazoned with a communist star. It's long been part of automotive history that the Soviets created the ZIS-110 by reverse engineering a 1942 Packard 180, so the gift by Stalin of a Packard earlier was not so coincidental.

In one sign of the economic and technological differences between capitalist and communist countries in the Cold War era, the placard next to a 1976 Cadillac DeVille states that it was given to the museum and no longer driven because of its "wastefulness." Some of the extravagant features listed include a "large eight-cylinder motor . . . and numerous electrical devices: seat-setting, wing mirror setting, control door lock etc. It also has a small light which lights up the door lock when you want to open it." Before this symbol of

American decadence was relegated to the museum, it was used by politicians of the Assembly of Yugoslavia who presumably had no problem with all the added amenities.

All is not luxury here though. On the second floor many daily drivers from the likes of Renault and Citroen are displayed. In my travels to car museums, I rarely come across a Yugo; the product of Yugoslavia's ill-fated attempt to crack the American compact car market. But there's a red one here. Although not seen any more on the road, the car lives on in popular folklore. The oldest maintained car in Slovenia is also displayed: a German-built 1906 Piccolo two-seater. Considering the armed struggles over the years in this region, it's a real survivor.

An exhibit produced with the Slovenian energy company, Petrol, highlights a pre-war filling station and vintage gas pumps. Outside in the courtyard there's a display of farm equipment that includes the wonderfully named Bubba tractor, a make from Italy. Before leaving, it's also worth taking some time to stroll the grounds where an antique water-powered sawmill that harkens back to the pre-motor age that is on display.

Technical Museum of Slovenia Bistra pri Vrhniki 6, Bistra, 1360 Vrhnika, Slovenia
www.tms.si

Note: Because the auto collection is just a part of the entire complex, you can easily spend a day here.

United Kingdom

Manual Labor at the Haynes International Motor Museum

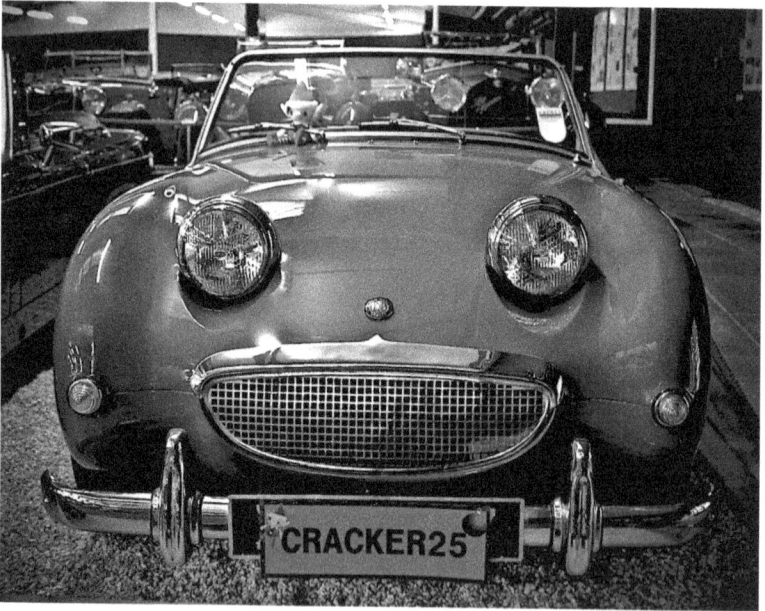

Haynes International Motor Museum Sparkford

When John Haynes was 16 years old, he purchased two Austin 7s and proceeded to salvage them to create his own sports car. What car-loving teenager hasn't tinkered around in the garage? Haynes was a little different though, taking his early interest to the next level. He founded the Haynes Publishing Group, creating the detailed car manuals – with their iconic yellow and red stripe – that are famous worldwide.

Not content to "just" publish books about cars, Haynes wanted to collect cars too. From a modest starting point of twenty-nine cars, Haynes has gone on to amass a stellar collection of more than 400 vehicles that form the heart of the Haynes International Motor Museum in Sparkford, England. Founded in 1985 on the remains of an American World War II-era ammunition dump, it's located about 120 miles west of London and is easily reachable by car or mass transit. Haynes calls it, "a sanctuary for 'petrol-heads' to immerse themselves in automotive history." With the oldest vehicle being an original condition 1897 Daimler Wagonette, that history starts early.

From that humble beginning the collection rambles from the dawn of motoring history through exotic supercars of today. Former museum curator Mike Penn emphasized that the Haynes is "a living museum where the cars still run and visitors can hear, touch, and smell them." In fact, they even built an adjacent test track to take them out for a spin.

Given John Haynes' early background getting his hands dirty working on cars, rather than just admiring them, Penn states, "there is an emphasis on the engines that power these machines."

The first exhibit highlights the birth of the piston engine with a quote from the famous 13th-century philosopher Roger Bacon, who lived just six miles from the museum's site: "One day chariots will be constructed which will start and move without the impulsion of man or horse, or any other animal." Other exhibits include videos and models of working engines to explain how they work.

The museum is broken out into several large halls. Given the location, there is an emphasis on British marques including Jaguar, Lotus, Morgan, Aston-Martin, Rover, and Jensen, dating back to the "glory days" of British automotive engineering.

One of the most popular cars greets visitors in the front lobby, a flaming red 1965 AC Cobra 289. It was one of Haynes's earliest purchases and has never been restored. About a decade ago the museum held a major show featuring 30 Cobras from across Europe. Carroll Shelby himself attended and drove this Cobra (at a gentle pace) on the test track, much to the delight of the gathered assemblage.

Because the museum has "International" in its name, they also feature many non-British brands. Some of the highlights include a 1972 Datsun 240Z, a 1992 Indian Hindustan Ambassador, and a beast of a Soviet 1959 Gaz M-13 Chaika that was modeled after a 1955 Packard Patrician.

Speaking of Detroit metal, the museum claims to have the largest collection of U.S.-built cars in the United Kingdom. A fine selection called "The American Dream" includes a 1928 Jordan Playboy, a rare 1920 Moon Model 642 Touring Car, and a 1937 Ford Model 78 Woody Wagon, among others. Pride of place goes to a 1931 Duesenberg Model J Derham Tourster.

One of the humblest galleries, and one of the most popular, is called Memory Lane. It features British daily drivers from the post-war years, causing many grandfathers to grow teary-eyed at the sight of a car from their early driving days, while exclaiming fondly, "Oh, I had one of these." In a museum stacked with, well, "museum pieces," it's refreshing to see so many accessible cars that visitors can remember riding in, including a 1960 Austin Nash Metropolitan, which tried (and failed) to be a hit in the US market; a 1967 Humber Hawk and the low-budget 1959 Ford Popular. Due to a design flaw the windshield wipers would stop working when the car accelerated; a quirk which made it not very popular after all.

A feast for the eyes is the Red Room, where dozens of red vehicles are lined up cheek to jowl. The curvaceous 1956 AC Ace Bristol looks familiar to any Cobra fan while the 1959 Austin Healey Frogeye (or Bugeye to Americans) Sprite became an affordable, and popular, sports car.

Other galleries include Minis and Micros, Motorcycle Mezzanine, Custom and Bespoke, the Morris Story (dedicated to the "M" in MG), Supercar Century, and more.

Haynes International Museum Sparkford, Yeovil BA22 7LH
www.HaynesMotorMuseum.com

London Hauling: A Dose of Double Deckers

London Bus Museum at Brooklands Weybridge
London Transport Museum London

For almost a century, one of the most iconic sights of London has been that of red double-decker buses plying the city's streets. The most famous is the Routemaster; it debuted in 1956 with sinewy lines and an open rear deck.

The glory of the city's busing is on display at the London Transport Museum is conveniently located at tourist-laden Covent Garden in the center of London. Here, the history of transporting people and goods around the capital dating back to 1800 is on view in the cast iron and brick structure that once housed the Victorian-era Flower Market. The soaring ceilings and skylights make it a perfect venue for displaying the tall red motorcoaches.

The oldest motorized bus in the museum is a 1908 Leyland X2 that is also the oldest surviving British-built bus. It represents an experiment at the time, transitioning from horse power to motor power which, ironically, would be measured in horses. An example of London's first successfully mass-produced motor buses – the 1911 B-Type Motorbus – spent time overseas. More than 1,000 of these served roles on the Continent during World War I as troop transports, ambulances, and mobile carrier pigeon lofts. This one returned to London after the war and was used while still in its wartime khaki livery.

The Routemaster became a well-known symbol of London as visitors flocked there during the 1960s Jet Age. Its clean lines were the product of industrial designer Douglas Scott, who was also responsible for the AGA cooker. The relatively lightweight bus employed interchangeable aluminum parts that were produced using expertise developed building airplanes during World War II. It was also the first bus with independent front suspension, power steering, and an automatic transmission. On view is a 1963 Routemaster.

The father of the Routemaster was the RT bus – the version here is from 1954. After the advent of the 1939 prototype, almost 7,000 were built, more than double that of the Routemaster, making it the most produced bus in history.

Along with motorized buses, the museum contains examples of horse-powered omnibuses, early railroad cars and a few taxis, as well as transport ephemera. Be sure to check out the separate ID badges for drivers marked "Animal Power" and "Mechanical Power," reflecting the introduction of new motorized technologies.

Due to space constraints at this site, most of the collection is located at the Museum Depot at Acton, a 30-minute Tube ride west of the museum. There you'll find the original Routemaster RM1 prototype that debuted at the Commercial Motor Show in 1954. The Acton facility is only open to the public on three select weekends throughout the year.

For another look at British busing heritage, head 25 miles southwest of London via railway to the Brooklands Museum. This attraction featuring motoring and aviation heritage (including a Concorde) is on the site of the original circa 1907 Brooklands race track, considered the birthplace of British motorsports. Visitors can still climb the steep incline of one of the surviving banked turns.

Other attractions at Brooklands include a wonderful car collection focusing on racing that includes: a 1912 Lorraine Dietrich Vieux Charles III that raced in the fourth ever Grand Prix; a 1937 Delahaye 135 S Competition Roadster that was crowned the world's fastest sports car at Brooklands in 1939; and a 1933 Napier-Railton that set many world endurance records.

Aviation sights include a re-creation of the 1930s Brooklands Aircraft Factory and the world's only working Concorde Flight Simulator. You can also tour an actual Concorde.

But we're here today for the buses so it's off to another on-site attraction: the London Bus Museum, where three dozen buses are arrayed among dioramas of London street scenes. It's a working museum with an active restoration shop and the buses are properly maintained and periodically taken out for a run.

The 1925 Dennis 4-ton has a second deck that is open to the elements, a surprising feature considering the London climate. Retired in 1931, the body was discovered in 1970 being used as a storage shed, a function it had served ever since it was taken off the road. It was restored with a correct chassis and subsequently embarked on a 2,000-mile tour of Japan. A later life as a movie star has had it appearing in films like 2018's *Mary Poppins Returns*.

A 1938 AEC Regal I coach bus sports green livery as it ran on the Green Line, a step up in comfort from regular bus service. During World War II it was pressed into local service as an ambulance after the Green Line was suspended. In later years it was downgraded into bus service and painted the familiar red. However, the museum has restored it to its illustrious green livery.

The 1 ½-deck 1953 AEC Regal IV in the blue-and-white livery of British European Airways is a rare sight. For two decades it was used to ferry passengers to Heathrow Airport; the extra half-deck provided space for luggage storage. It was eventually replaced by traditional Routemasters that towed luggage trailers.

For a taste of these great buses in action, during a visit to London, board a red double-decker bus, climb to the top level and grab a seat in front to sightsee around town and experience the joy of London buses as they were originally intended.

London Bus Museum Brooklands Drive, Weybridge, Surrey, KT13 0SL, UK
www.LondonBusMuseum.com
and www.BrooklandsMuseum.com

London Transport Museum Covent Garden Piazza, London WC2E 7BB, UK
www.LTMuseum.co.uk

Note: If your travel plans don't include jetting across the Atlantic any time soon, the **Museum of Bus Transportation**, located inside the AACA Museum in Hershey, PA, provides an up-close look at American busing history. From an evolving collection, around a dozen buses are usually on display ranging from a 1927 Fageol "Safety Coach" through a 1986 GM T8H-5307A "Fishbowl" that is one of the few survivors that appeared in the film Speed – it's the last GM "New Look" that was built. There's also a 1959 GMC that had a star turn in *Forrest Gump*. Cabinets filled with bus models featuring livery from transit lines across the country round out the collection. See more at www.BusMuseum.org

The Wonderful World of Beaulieu at a Downton Abbey Style Estate

National Motor Museum at Beaulieu Hampshire

Imagine a destination in the English countryside that contains an internationally renowned car museum, lush, manicured gardens, an abbey right out of, well, Downton Abbey, a palatial mansion, and a spy museum, all connected by a monorail whose idea was inspired by Expo '67 in Montreal, and you have an idea of what awaits on your visit to Beaulieu.

Set in deep wooded terrain 90 miles southwest of London, this potpourri of an attraction was assembled, starting in the 1950s, by Lord Montagu of Beaulieu (pronounced "Bew-lee"), whose family has occupied these grounds since King Henry VIII granted them in 1538.

Lord Montagu, who died in 2015 at the age of 88, was part Walt Disney, part P. T. Barnum, and part James Bond (the debonair David Niven version). In 1952 he was among the first of the landed gentry to open his great house to the public. Although originally considered déclassé by the other aristocracy for his actions, Lord Montagu was in fact a trendsetter. His prescient vision allowed him to keep the expensive and unwieldy estate in the family; others, seeing his success, eventually followed suit.

The Palace House has been the residence of the Montagu family and their ancestors since 1538. Originally the gatehouse for the Abbey, with 19th-century embellishments it's now a cross between a medieval castle and an English country estate. Inside, the Gothic rib-vaulted ceilings of the spacious rooms do justice to the term "cathedral ceiling."

Although there are still residences upstairs, visitors are allowed to roam far throughout the home, giving a true feel for being the lord of the manse. Highlights include the Art Russe gallery (devoted to Soviet-era Russian art) and Lord Montagu's wonderful library.

In 2017, the kitchen was restored to its Victorian-era appearance to demonstrate cooking of that period. It's very much a working kitchen though, as evidenced by the current Lord Montagu's cook's shortbread cookies for sale in the gift shop.

But it hasn't always been tea and crumpets at Beaulieu. During World War II, the grounds played a key role in the war effort. The estate's location just off the English Channel made it strategically important. The British Special Operations Executive set up a "Finishing School" for special agents' final training as they prepared to parachute behind enemy lines and join up with local Resistance groups. "Secret Army," is an exhibit on the grounds devoted to their dangerous efforts. During the war, the adjacent village became a "no go" zone for civilians as agents trained for their clandestine activities.

Within steps of the Palace House are the well-preserved remains of the original 13th-century Beaulieu Abbey. Ordered destroyed by King Henry VIII during his dissolution of monasteries, it has been preserved over the years by the Montagu family and its ancestors, it now houses exhibits related to daily life of the Cistercian monks who inhabited it.

The pride of Beaulieu is the National Motor Museum located on the grounds. Lord Montagu started it as a small display of pre-World War I cars in tribute to his father, John, the Second Baron of Montagu, who at the turn of the last century was an early advocate of a new-fangled invention called the automobile – even introducing the royal family to the concept. But in the way of these things, what started as a small collection grew into the 250-vehicle leviathan it is today.

Cars range from the oldest Renault, an 1899 model, through a 2010 Ferrari 599 GTO that's claimed to be the fastest road car ever, clocking in at 208 mph. Historic photos portray the early days of motoring, when it was considered so dangerous that someone had to walk in front of the car waving a red flag to warn pedestrians, lest they be run over by the blustery contraption.

A special exhibit titled "For Britain & For the Hell of It" highlights the nation's influence on the world of speed. On display are racing machines that set land speed records in the continual competition between American and British drivers. The scarlet éclair-shaped 1,000 horsepower Sunbeam was the first car to exceed 200 miles per hour; it achieved this goal in 1927 (!). The car museum can keep a visitor occupied for hours, which is not a problem when there is so much else to see here.

But back to that monorail, which kids of all ages will love. Not only does it glide overhead outside, connecting the main attractions at Beaulieu, but it also hovers along just beneath the rooftop *inside* the National Motor Museum, giving the proverbial bird's-eye view of the cars, while also conveying the keen vision and showmanship of Lord Montagu.

National Motor Museum Beaulieu, New Forest, Hampshire, SO42 7ZN www.beaulieu.co.uk

Note: There is so much to see that a return visit within 6 days is free.

Great Scots: Classic Cars in Glasgow and Edinburgh

Riverside Museum Glasgow & **National Museum of Scotland** Edinburgh

With a strong industrial heritage, Scotland was an early player in the automotive world. Much of this history is on display at two museums, the Riverside Museum in Glasgow, and the National Museum of Scotland in Edinburgh. The former highlights all forms of transportation while the latter includes transportation, technology and, for those not automotive inclined, artwork and natural science exhibits.

Riverside Museum, Glasgow

The Riverside Museum sits at the junction of the Kelvin and Clyde Rivers. The latter was the launching site of the RMS *Queen Mary* liner and the doomed HMS Hood battle cruiser. The building itself, with its jagged façade poking into the sky, is an ode to Glasgow's legacy of ship building and train manufacturing. It opened in 2011 with a 3,000-piece collection of transportation items including classic cars, a world-famous wooden ship model collection, vintage bicycles, motorcycles, locomotives, double-decker buses and more.

The car collection is displayed unlike any I've ever seen, with many of them precariously resting on shelves jutting out three stories high from the wall. While about half the cars are at ground level, so you can walk around them and peer into them, not so for the ones dangling above. It's kind of an odd juxtaposition. The cars appear to be so far away that they can convincingly look like someone's collection of Matchbox cars.

Scotland may not be as well known for wide scale automotive manufacturing as England is, but several cars built here in the early days of motoring are given pride of place on the ground floor.

An early success story in Scotland was Argyll Motors, Ltd. Founded in 1899, it was soon producing more than 800 cars per year making it a leading European car manufacturer. Befitting its reputation as a luxury marque, the Argyll factory, located about 15 miles northwest of Glasgow, was likened to a palace with marble staircases, deluxe bathrooms, and a gilded dome.

Perhaps it makes sense then that the cars, with their embossed leatherwork, and gold-trimmed seating, were affordable only to a thin slice of the market. By 1908 Argyll Motors was deep in debt and not profitable enough. They continued to try to sell to the luxury buyer but eventually went bankrupt.

The Argyll may have been unsuccessful partially due to its high price, but Ford achieved success in Great Britain making affordable cars. The 1955 Ford Popular 103E was Britain's lowest price car when it debuted two years earlier. They were so, well, popular, they achieved cult status by being mocked in a classic Monty Python skit *Mr. and Mrs. Brian Norris' Ford Popular.*

Another practical set of wheels is the 1963 Hillman Imp, whose name confirms its stature. The rear aluminum engine car was a rival to the Mini. According to a *Popular Mechanics* review at the time, "the swing-out action reminds you that 62 percent of the weight is on the rear wheels." Surprisingly, it became a popular rally car.

An example of how homespun early cars were is the 1901 Arrol-Johnston dogcart, a horse-drawn cart that carried hunting dogs for the aristocratic set when they went on the hunt. Clever car designers placed an engine in place of the dog basket and – voilà – a new automobile was born.

The 1904 Albion A3 tonneau, with upgrades like a windshield and inflatable inner tubes for the tires, shows the evolution of the automobile in the early years of motoring from that dogcart.

Anyone visiting London has noticed the ubiquitous black taxi cabs with their long hoods and boxy shape that look like they were plucked out of a 1930's film set. The forerunner for these vehicles were produced by Beardmore Motors in Paisley, Scotland, which is considered the birthplace of the London cab. The design of the 1932 Beardmore Mark III Hyper taxi on display is a result of the stringent *Conditions of Fitness*, including a tight turning radius and higher ground clearance, that London authorities required for taxis to operate on the city's crowded streets, features that eventually made their way into civilian cars.

The 1905 Rolls-Royce is the luxury marque's second oldest survivor and one of only six cars they built that year. The sporty 1963 Volvo P1800 is the model made famous by Roger Moore in the TV series The Saint. The unibody shells were built in Scotland.

With funding from the British government, the 1977 Chrysler Sunbeam rear-drive hatchback was built at the former Rootes Group factory in Linwood, Scotland in the late '70s using a Hillman Avenger as a base. The sleek 1994 Haldane HD300 kit car, which was produced in Scotland from 1988 to 1994, evoked an Austin-Healey 3000 while using a Ford Pinto 2.0-liter engine and gearbox.

The cars displayed high up on the wall are heavy on Scottish built marques including a 1900 Argyll Voiture 5 hp, 1910 Albion A3 16 hp touring, 1913 Argyll 15/30 hp tourer and a 1920 Arrol-Johnston 15.9.

National Museum of Scotland, Edinburgh

The National Museum of Scotland is filled with galleries that befit a national museum including art, natural sciences, design and more. The modest automotive collection is tucked in a corner of the Science and Technology gallery where the Scottish penchant for stacking cars on a wall is once again evident. Formula 1 racing cars are piled three high including the Ferrari powered Red Bull RB02 that Scottish driver David Coulthard drove to Red Bull's first podium appearance in the 2006 F1 Monaco Grand Prix.

Pride of place on its own ground level podium goes to the bright red 1910 Argyll Flying Fifteen. Magazine advertisements of the period boasted of Argyll's "reputation for high class quality and workmanship that have made the name Argyll world-famous." Unfortunately, Argyll was on its last legs by then. Founder Alex Govan died in 1907 and his huge investment in a new factory to copy American mass production techniques had failed. The company shut down in 1908 only to be resurrected in two years with the Flying Fifteen but, despite Argyll's reputation for quality, that venture was not successful either.

However, the Argyll marque lives on at the Riverside Museum in Glasgow and the National Museum of Scotland in Edinburgh as an example of early Scottish automotive ingenuity.

Riverside Museum Pointhouse Place, Glasgow, G3 8RS Scotland
www.glasgowlife.org.uk/museums/venues/riverside-museum

National Museum of Scotland Chambers Street, Edinburgh, EH1 1JF Scotland
www.nms.ac.uk/national-museum-of-scotland

NORTH AMERICA

CANADA

TAKING VISITORS BACK IN TIME
DOWN GASOLINE ALLEY

GASOLINE ALLEY Calgary

After a long road trip across the plains of central Canada, where seemingly endless fields of wheat and canola are punctuated by a lone tree every few miles, entering Calgary's Gasoline Alley museum can be a bit overwhelming. From floor level to its three-story height ceiling the 75,000 square foot building, which is designed to look like the former Calgary Public Market, is adorned with thousands of objects that will appeal to collectors of both classic cars and petroliana.

It is a true gem whose mission is to provide visitors with "a celebration of industrial design illuminated by a storyline that follows the far-reaching social changes that resulted from the introduction and popularization of the automobile." The airplane-hangar-sized building is packed to the brim with automotive artifacts, plus a select collection of 60 classic cars and trucks that are not often found elsewhere. The timeline of the collection is from the turn of the last century through the 1950s.

In addition, scattered throughout are 146 antique gas pumps and globes that make up one of the largest collections of restored gas pumps in North America and give the museum its name.

The bulk of the collection was donated by local businessman Ron Carey. Decades before the popularity of shows like *American Pickers* and *Antiques Roadshow*, Carey searched the countryside seeking elusive barn finds for both undiscovered vehicles and automotive memorabilia. Eventually he had too much to store and donated his collection where it now forms the core of the museum.

Gasoline Alley is part of a larger attraction called Heritage Park, one of Canada's leading living history museums that focuses on the settlement of Western Canada. In that role, a historical village includes structures like an antique midway and saloon along with a vintage train that meanders throughout the 127-acre park. Heritage Park is closed after Canadian Thanksgiving through mid-May. Good news for classic car fans though: Gasoline Alley is located with a separate entrance right next to the parking lot and is open year-round.

The soaring wooden cathedral ceiling is decorated with neon and enamel signs from bygone days of automotive touring. One round sign emblazoned with a maple leaf marketed Supertest Petroleum, "Canada's All-Canadian Company." Other gasoline company signs from the past include those for Derby, Tydol Flying A, and Beacon Oil along with Imperial Marvelube, touted as the "Purest of Motor Oils."

It's no surprise that there are several Canadian-built vehicles in the collection. A 1909 McIntyre Model M may be the only restored one that survives. With a handcrafted body and tufted leather seats, it represented the company's heritage of fine carriage building. It also featured 36" wheels and an air-cooled four-cylinder engine.

A 1918 McLaughlin Buick was billed as "Canada's standard car" and was popular with Prohibition-era bootleggers while plying routes from British Columbia into Alberta and Montana at a time when British Columbia had repealed Prohibition sooner than in the States.

The 1922 Gray-Dort Model 19-B Touring Car was produced by Ontario-based Gray-Dort Motors. The project was a result of the Canadian Company Gray & Sons acquiring the rights to assemble cars designed by the Dort Motor Company of Flint, Michigan. Over a decade they produced 26,000 vehicles.

A rare 1927 Star Grain truck was one of the last Star trucks produced with a chassis built at the Durant Motor Company plant in Leaside, Ontario by the Canada Carriage & Body Company of Brantford, Ontario. (Or, as museum guide Bill Jones said, "down east.") However, it was underpowered and primarily used for light duty. Other trucks include the only known surviving 1912 Mack Senior truck, a 1916 Coffin-Nosed International, and a 1920 Autocar truck with a scissor-lift dump box.

The 1937 Hudson Terraplane Big Boy Pickup was so named because it was like "flying on land"; aviator Amelia Earhart was a proponent of the brand. With a waterfall grille and torpedo headlights that give it a sedan-like appearance, the one on view here is rather slick looking for a pickup; yet it still boasted a rugged frame that was suited for hauling.

It wasn't all rough terrain in Alberta, though, with several high-end sedans on display, including a 1931 Cord L-29 and 1932 Auburn V-12. The Cord was the first major American car with front-wheel drive. Despite its elegant rakish looks, the Auburn was a low-cost alternative to the Cord, costing the equivalent of only $15,000 today. A diminutive 1935 Austin Seven Nippy was nicknamed the "Baby Austin." This one was built in Australia on an English chassis.

Calgary was a beneficiary of newspaper publisher Horace Greeley's mid-19th century advice to "Go west, young man," as pioneers crossed the plains for the fertile farming grounds of Alberta. Skip ahead a century and that same recommendation was now sending people west in search of a holiday in the stunning Canadian Rockies in cars like the 1956 Plymouth Sport Suburban station wagon hauling a 1959 Champion Holiday Traveler caravan.

Since part of the museum's mission is to educate visitors about the settling of Western Canada, there are several farm vehicles on display. One of the oldest is the 1911 Chase Auto Delivery Wagon that functioned as a simple motorized farm wagon. Given its workload, not many of these are still intact.

Ron Carey and his crew have beautifully restored most of the items he unearthed. However, a few are kept in their original unrestored condition to illustrate how they were used. One example is a 1924 International Truck that, with its rusted chassis and rough wooden cab, looks like it's barely standing, but also attests to the sturdiness of these hard-working machines.

Alberta is also an oil and gas producing province so petroliana fits right in here. Some examples are in the Husky Gallery, located in a recreated Husky service station; it's packed full of service station artifacts along with vintage auto parts and head lamps in their original boxes. Wooden shelves are lined with antique gas pump globes with names like Koolmotor High Test Anti Knock Gasoline; Puro Pep, The Pure Oil; White Rose Ethyl and a rare one for Green Streak. The collection surrounds a 1915 Cadillac that was retrofitted in 1922 as a rather high-style tow truck. It's parked next a 1905 Cadillac in its rough as-fund condition.

The museum contains perhaps the largest collection of vintage gas pumps and globes in North America. Emblazoned with colorful names like Artic Ethyl, Violet Ray Anti-Knock Gasoline and Red Crown, the fragile glass globes that sat atop the pump marketing the product contained inside provide historical records of bygone companies that helped early motorists ply the roads.

Like the car companies themselves, the gas companies issued new designs of pumps every year, creating a staggering number of pump models that have grown into their own segment of the car collecting hobby. Unlike today, where gas stations carry a single brand with different grades of product, older style pumps carried multiple brands. A customer (or, more likely, an attendant) twisted a handle on the pump that would select the brand of choice.

Calgary began as a small farming and cattle community in the late 19th century and then became an important center for the petroleum industry following the discovery of natural gas just outside of town in 1914 – it hasn't looked back since. A visit to Gasoline Alley provides a fascinating look at the artifacts of the city's energy-based economy, which came of age just as automobiles themselves were becoming mainstream in society. It will appeal to anyone interested in antique cars, trucks and petroliana, along with a particular emphasis on Canadian history.

Gasoline Alley 1900 Heritage Park SW, Calgary, Alberta T2V 2X3, Canada
    www.HeritagePark.ca

Heavy Metal Tundra:
Uncovering Canadian Classics in Manitoba

Jim's Vintage Garages Headingley, Manitoba
Manitoba Antique Automobile Museum Elkhorn, Manitoba

As I took a road trip across Canada, I realized how classic car happy our neighbors to the north are. Rolling across the wide-open landscape it wasn't unusual to spot a Model T, a 1950s land yacht or Mopar muscle car out for a summer drive. This love of all things vintage is apparent at two car museums in Manitoba: the Manitoba Antique Automobile Museum in Elkhorn and Jim's Vintage Garages on the outskirts of Winnipeg.

Manitoba Antique Automobile Museum

The Manitoba Antique Automobile Museum is a time capsule of the first half of the 20th century in Canada. Most of the 70 cars are in their "as found" condition from more than a half-century ago. As is so often the case, the museum began as a private collection, but for a unique purpose. After the end of World War II many automobiles were sent to the crusher to make up for a steel shortage. An area farmer named Isaac Clarkson was concerned that local history was being obliterated along with the cars, so he started buying up old vehicles. Many were true "barn finds," rusting near hay bales or out in a field, which Clarkson acquired for a few dollars each. Along the way he acquired dozens of cars, including a 1908 REO, 1909 Hupmobile (the first car Clarkson saved and restored), 1908 Overland, 1908 Metz, and a 1930 American Austin.

The collection really shines in the output of the McLaughlin Motor Car Company of Ontario. Sam McLaughlin was an early Canadian automotive pioneer, transforming the family carriage company into an automobile manufacturer. He set up a joint venture with General Motors, initially using mostly Buick components in his cars. There are seven McLaughlins on display, ranging from a 1910 McLaughlin Model 8 to a 1917 McLaughlin Model D-45.

Highlighting the local homespun nature of the museum, guide Richard Hainer recalls the time a 90-year-old visitor pointed out that the actual 1910 McLaughlin in the collection was his father's car. A month later his sister rolled into the museum in her wheelchair and declared, "I'm here to see my dad's car." The 1912 E-M-F 30 on display is from the Detroit-based car company that in 1911 was second only to Ford in sales. Due to reliability issues, the initials soon stood for "Every Morning Fix-it," among other epithets.

While most of the cars don't run, a few models that were added to the museum later are kept in running condition for parades. These include a Mercury-derived Canadian-built 1954 Monarch Lucerne. It reveals its Canadian roots with the three gold maple leaves in the logo. Another "crossover" vehicle is the 1968 Meteor Montcalm, which is also part of the Mercury family tree. Original framed magazine advertisements for the cars are set next to them showing their original prices and selling points.

An automotive bone yard out back contains approximately 50 vehicles, some of which are for sale. Most striking is the collection of mid-century Fargo trucks from Chrysler, with their swirling rust patterns looking like a psychedelic form of flames. The museum is open daily from May 1 through September 30.

Jim's Vintage Garages

Continue on the Trans-Canada Highway three hours due east to the Royal Municipality of Headingley. Here you'll come across Jim's Vintage Garages, a museum devoted to preserving the history of the petroleum industry in Canada. The collection was created by Jim and Vivienne Pearn, who donated their collection of petroliana to the township in 2004, where it now resides in a dedicated space in the community center.

Inside visitors will find replicas of six vintage service stations. Each "station" represents a specific brand that was active in Canada including White Rose, Red Indian, and Imperial Esso. The meticulously curated vignettes hold shelves with tools of the trade: spark plugs, oil cans, uniforms, license plates, peg boards full of hub caps and hub cap wrenches, along with walls plastered with vintage signs. It's the first museum where I've found a wooden frame holding tools that is emblazoned Grease Guns of the '20s or a box full of Carter Carburetor parts.

To complete the authentic look, members of the Manitoba Classic & Antique Auto Club have loaned the museum ten antique cars and motorcycles that are scattered among the service stations. The museum is such a trip back in time that I half expected a fellow in overalls to stride through the door, wiping his greasy hands on a rag as he asked me what I thought of that up-and-coming local hockey phenom, Gordie Howe. On a visit you might find a 1910 Harley-Davidson motorcycle, 1926 International Harvester oil tanker, or a 1934 Maple Leaf truck; the latter was produced in Canada by Chevrolet and is embellished with maple leaf logos.

The museum is generally open from June through September.

In northern Manitoba, on Hudson Bay, polar bears prowl roads of their own making. Farther south in the province, the classic car culture is alive and well, with vintage motors prowling manmade roads at hundreds of cruises and car shows throughout the summer months. If you're visiting the region, the Manitoba Association of Auto Clubs publishes a comprehensive annual guide to car shows in the province. To download a digital version, go to www.maac.cc.

Manitoba Antique Automobile Museum Trans-Canada Hwy, Elkhorn, MB R0M 0N0, Canada

www.facebook.com/ManitobaAntiqueAutomoblieMuseum

Jim's Vintage Garages 5353 Portage Ave. West, Headingley, MB R4H 1J9, Canada

www.jimsvintagegarages.ca

EASTERN UNITED STATES

Sᴡᴇᴇᴛ Rɪᴅᴇs: Tᴜᴄᴋᴇʀs, Bᴜsᴇs ᴀɴᴅ ᴍᴏʀᴇ ɪɴ Hᴇʀsʜᴇʏ

AACA Mᴜsᴇᴜᴍ Hershey, Pennsylvania

People who grew up in the northeastern part of the United States know Hershey, Pennsylvania as the "Sweetest Place on Earth" due to the presence of the Hershey Company factories. The town literally smelled like chocolate and the streetlights were even shaped like Hershey's Kisses. Speaking personally, that was all very exciting for a chubby eight-year-old who knew his way around a candy store.

Flash forward a few decades and I now look forward to a visit to Hershey so I can see what's new at the AACA Museum. Opened in 2003, the museum sprawls over three floors with a collection comprised of vehicles that have been donated or are on loan. It is affiliated with the Smithsonian Institution, a rare achievement for a car museum.

Additionally, the museum houses the Cammack Tucker Collection, the world's most extensive collection of Tucker Automobiles and memorabilia; the Museum of Bus Transportation; a collection of more than 300 radiator mascots; a rambling "O" gauge model train display; and a huge collection of vintage road maps. Every year from May through October there is a special exhibit related to motorcycles. So there really is something for everyone.

There are usually 80 to 100 vehicles on display – some from the collection of more than 150 and some on loan – at any one time. The oldest is an 1895 Chicago Motor Benton Harbor that is car #20 on the National Historic Vehicle Register.

Moving forward in time, one car here that many of us lusted after in high school is the 1978 Datsun 280Z with a larger bore 2.8-liter L28 engine. Although what was up with that space saver spare tire? The concept, which had originated in the aerospace industry, was still revolutionary in cars and not something neighborhood motorheads readily embraced.

Cammack Tucker Gallery

The Cammack Tucker Gallery is truly special. Of the 51 iconic 1948 Tuckers that were produced, around 20 are normally on public display in the United States. With this limited amount, it's quite incredible to find that the AACA Museum boasts three of them: #1001, #1022, and #1026. The latter is a rare automatic transmission Tucker. The gallery also contains the world's largest collection of Tucker memorabilia and company archives.

Long-time Tucker enthusiast David Cammack generously bequeathed his collection to the museum. Over time he purchased the Tuckers along with prototype engines, spare parts and the surviving books and records of the company, including personal correspondence of Preston Tucker.

Many of these records are on display in wooden slide-out cases. The scope of the collection is incredible and yields many hidden treasures for a Tucker fan. Open one drawer and you may see official company photos from the car's launch, slide open another and gaze upon original sketches of the Tucker logo.

There's a full-sized Waltz Blue fiberglass mock-up of a Tucker front end built by custom-car crafter and Tucker enthusiast Ron Ida. The headlights work and a curved wall in front of the mock-up lets visitors turning the steering wheel witness the sweeping effect of the Tucker's "Cyclops" center headlight as it turned corners.

Tucker bought the Franklin Engine Company and tinkered with their aircraft engines for his car. Engines on display including several prototypes that never made it into the car and a rare 166 horsepower Tucker R-1-2 engine with an automatic tranny. It was salvaged from Tucker #1042, the only other one that was an automatic, which had been destroyed.

The Tucker legacy lives on at the museum in other ways too. According to Preston Tucker's grandson, AACA Board Member John R. Tucker, Jr, "My sons and I continue to be involved in many aspects of the Cammack display. We are very active in rotating displays and bringing out new items."

Museum of Bus Transportation

The Museum of Bus Transportation, located downstairs, is a unique find. More than 50 buses include a 1959 GM Coach that was featured in Forrest Gump. The 21-passenger capacity 1912 White Truck was an early motor coach purchased for the Pennsylvania-based White Transit Company. It featured flame-lit headlights.

PBS news anchor Jim Lehrer, who passed away in 2020, was an avid bus memorabilia collector. His father was a bus driver who briefly owned the Kansas Central Lines bus company in the 1940s before it went bankrupt after one year. In 1989 Lehrer and his wife Kate purchased the 1946 Flxible Clipper on display, which they liveried in the colors of his father's defunct bus line.

Rotating Exhibits

Because the museum runs multiple temporary exhibits throughout the year in addition to its permanent collection, there's always something new to see. During my most recent visit they were winding down the special displays "Keep On Truckin': Light-Duty Trucks," "Minibike Mania" and "Iconic Chevrolets."

Other exhibits have included "Survivors: Unrestored Classic Cars, Trucks, & Motorcycles," featuring vehicles that have not been altered in any way, and "Packards Presented by Keystone Packards," a regional Packard club. Since the collection of cars and special exhibits change throughout the year, if there is a particular vehicle you want to see check their website. Also check their schedule for the popular Model T Driving Experience where students get to spend four hours learning how to drive a Model T.

Nearby auto attractions

If you're heading to Hershey, the swap meets at Carlisle are only 45 minutes away so you never know what you might pick up. (CarlisleEvents.com) And if you made it that far, the Swigart Museum in Huntingdon, PA, home of two Tuckers including the Tin Goose prototype, is just under two hours northwest of Carlisle, giving you the opportunity to see five (!) Tuckers in one day. (SwigartMuseum.com)

On the way out of the AACA Museum take a look at the Kissmobile parked by the front entrance. With its trio of 12-foot-high Hershey's Kisses astride a 26-foot-long chassis, the Hershey's version of the Oscar Meyer Weinermobile truly defines a sweet ride.

AACA Museum 161 Museum Drive, Hershey, PA 17033
www.aacamuseum.org

From Buggies to Mister Softee in Pennsylvania

Boyertown Museum of Historic Vehicles Boyertown, PA

Founded in 1965, the Boyertown Museum of Historic Vehicles is an extensive collection that includes gasoline, steam, and electric powered cars along with carriages and sleighs. The main exhibit area occupies the former factory of the Boyertown Auto Body Works, where truck bodies were built from 1926 through 1990. A few of these trucks have returned home and are now on display. Located 50 miles northwest of Philadelphia, the museum's focus is on Pennsylvania-built cars, reflecting the Keystone State's importance in the early automobile industry. There's also a connection with automotive pioneer Charles Duryea who set up shop nearby.

A showpiece of the museum is the 1872 Hill, one of the earliest autos in existence. Teenager James Hill built it just up the road in Fleetwood. Ironically, given the name of the inventor, the first model was too weak to climb hills. The 1913 S.G.V. Touring Car was built in nearby Reading and originally featured a steering wheel mounted pushbutton Vulcan Electric Gear Shift. Unfortunately, the wildly named technology was ahead of its time and malfunctioned repeatedly, causing the cars to be retrofitted with a floor mounted shift.

A 1915 Biddle with dual side-mounted wire wheels was manufactured in Philadelphia, one of only five believed to exist. The rakish cream-colored 1918 Biddle Roadster looks like it could race on the streets right now.

Six Duryeas manufactured in southeastern Pennsylvania are on display including a Philadelphia-built 1917 Duryea GEM Roadster, a three-wheeled hybrid of motorcycle and car. It was a sales flop and Charles Duryea's last attempt at automobile production. At least the GEM came with a steering wheel, unlike the joystick steering on the other Duryeas. The stubborn car builder didn't like steering wheels and was late to the game in using them.

The extensive bicycle collection highlights how many car companies grew out of bicycle manufacturers; in an intriguing setup there are two bicycles from the Acme Bicycle Manufacturing Company alongside a 1910 Acme Roadster.

The 1952 Masano is a unique car built by Reading, PA auto dealer Tom Masano. Its one-off fiberglass body is mated with a Henry J chassis Masano found in a junkyard – what's most striking is the triple tail fin configuration straddling the trunk. It was the first fiberglass bodied car to be licensed in Pennsylvania.

A crowd favorite is a 1958 Ford Mister Softee Ice Cream Truck that blared the ubiquitous theme song around the neighborhood of my youth. They were all fabricated in this building.

The oldest attraction is the restored 1872 Jeremiah Sweinhart Carriage Factory; it was the launching pad for the Boyertown vehicle industry. Inside you'll find a reconstructed blacksmith shop and belt-driven machine shop which still works. Several carriages are on display including one of the museum's oldest pieces, an 1875 Hose Cart that was used by the local fire company which, not looking bad for its age, now resides in the shop where it was built.

The museum also features roadside architecture including a 1921 Sun Oil cottage-style service station and the 1938 Fegely's Reading Diner. During periodic Diner Days, visitors can sit down in the diner and order a cup of coffee and slice of pie at 1930s prices. A must-see event is the annual Duryea Day Antique, Classic Car and Truck Show that takes place Labor Day weekend and attracted over 700 entrants last year.

For an auto-related detour, head 15 miles northwest to the small hamlet of Fleetwood, former home of Fleetwood Metal Auto Body. Founded in 1909, Fleetwood built coaches for Packard, Pierce-Arrow, Cadillac, and other high-end brands. Fisher Body Company/General Motors acquired it in 1925, moving the operations to Detroit within six years. The Fleetwood name was long associated with Cadillac models until it was retired in the 1990s. Visiting Fleetwood today you'll still find an original manufacturing building marked "1909 Fleetwood Auto Bodies" at the corner of Locust and South Franklin Streets as a tribute to that long ago legacy.

Boyertown Museum of Historic Vehicles 85 South Walnut Street, Boyertown, PA 19512
www.BoyertownMuseum.org

An Eastern Shore Museum Encourages the Next Generation of Classic Car Buffs

Classic Motor Museum St. Michael's, Maryland

It's always exciting to witness the birth of a car museum. Not only does it offer the possibility of unearthing a forgotten classic vehicle, but it also demonstrates that interest in the hobby is alive and well, and ready to coach a new crop of enthusiasts. Such is the case with the Classic Motor Museum of St. Michaels, which opened in 2017 on the bucolic Eastern Shore of Maryland.

"The museum's mission is to educate the next generation about auto restoration and give back to the community," says executive director Linda Haddaway King. "Our plan is to add automotive restoration classes to the career technology education classes offered at the local high school. In February, with 11 students, we formed the Classic Motor Museum Student Chapter of the AACA, which was just recognized at their annual meeting." The students have been restoring a 1938 Alvis under the discerning eye of museum president Tad duPont, who is rarely seen without a chamois cloth in his hand to wipe errant fingerprints off the cars on display. The goal is a Concours-level restoration, which is appropriate for a town that hosts an annual Concours d'Elegance each September.

The 21-car collection resides in an Amish-built barn-like structure just steps from the downtown retail core of St. Michaels. According to duPont, "So far there hasn't really been a theme because we're so new. The locals have been very generous about providing cars and some come from farther away as people discover us. Some are on loan, some are promised, and some are donated."

The variety changes regularly as local owners pick up one car they have on display as they drop off another, so there are new cars to see on each visit. With a small collection, the museum tries to offer something for everyone. It's not unusual to view a 1934 Auburn Speedster sitting next to a 1969 Oldsmobile 442, while the oldest vehicle is a 1910 International Harvester Model A Auto Buggy.

DuPont says, "Everybody's had a first car and whenever I ask – would they like to have their first car back? – they all say yes." So, the 442 is joined by a 1966 GTO and a 1967 Chevy Camaro in a corner of the museum that could be sub-titled "the ones that got away." The red 1964 Chevrolet Corvair Monza convertible reminds one how beautiful and unique these cars were. The 1941 Buick Super Eight convertible is just begging to be taken to the open road with the top down. Since all the cars here run, it will soon get that opportunity.

Pride-of-place belongs to a 1938 Bugatti Type 57 Stelvio Cabriolet, which had just been delivered on the day of my visit. Gangloff of Colmar, France built the body. This was the first year that Bugatti's son Jean successfully prevailed on his father to install more reliable hydraulic brakes, unlike earlier models that used cable brakes. Ettore Bugatti did not trust hydraulics, stating his cars were made to go, not stop.

Also, from across the pond, there's a pair of flame red MGs, a 1949 MG YT and 1953 MG TF. The color matches nicely with an actual fire engine, a 1931 American LaFrance, on which visitors are encouraged to ring the bell and climb aboard for a photo op. Plans are afoot to take people out for a ride on it.

To put the cars in context, placards that highlight historical details accompany them. For example, the 1934 Ford Deluxe notes that it's the same make and year car in which bank robbers Bonnie and Clyde were killed. The 1922 Packard Open Touring Car appeared in the HBO series *Boardwalk Empire*.

Coinciding with the Concours d'Elegance, the museum hosts their own Autofest. According to duPont, "The Autofest is for everybody. While the Concours is high-end and very specific, this will appeal to everyone, from Model Ts to Corvettes and really anything." The museum also has an extensive Classroom and Library that will help educate the next generation of car buffs with hands-on education geared towards classic car restoration.

Classic Motor Museum of St. Michaels 102 E. Marengo Street, St. Michaels, MD 21663

www.ClassicMotorMuseum.org

A Trio of Museums Celebrate
the Buckeye State's Automotive Heritage

Crawford Auto-Aviation Museum at the Cleveland History Center Cleveland, Ohio
National Packard Museum Warren, Ohio
America's Packard Museum Dayton, Ohio

In his song *Youngstown*, Bruce Springsteen refers to Northeast Ohio as an industrial powerhouse that won America's wars. In the early years of motoring the region was the nation's leading producer of cars and Cleveland was a contender to become the nation's Motor City. Detroit eventually earned that title, but Northeast Ohio's distinguished motoring heritage is celebrated at several museums, plus one in the southwest part of the state.

Cleveland Rocks

The Crawford Auto-Aviation Museum at the Cleveland History Center highlights the automotive past of the city overlooking Lake Erie. Nestled among the 140-car collection, Cleveland-produced cars include an 1899 Winton, 1902 American Gas, 1920 Jordan Playboy, and an appropriately named 1920 Cleveland whose "Body by Fisher" was also manufactured in town.

While the museum focuses on Northeast Ohio-manufactured vehicles, they also collect examples that demonstrate innovation in the auto industry. Accordingly, one of the highlights of the "REVolution" exhibit is an assemblage of shimmering stainless-steel cars. In the 1930s Ford teamed up with Allegheny Steel to produce six 1936 Ford Tudor sedans that were driven around the country as a promotional tool. One of them is on display, along with other stainless-steel cars, including a 1960 Thunderbird, 1966 Lincoln Continental convertible, and the obligatory DeLorean.

Since "Aviation" is in the title of the museum, a 1944 North American P-51K Mustang provides a nod to the Cleveland National Air Races of the 1920s through 1940s. The former fighter plane competed for the Thompson Trophy in 1946.

Alternative fuel vehicles include a 1916 Owen Magnetic that was sold as "The Car with a Thousand Speeds," due to its unique propulsion system. Built in Cleveland, the early hybrid combines the smooth operation of an electric motor with the power of a combustion engine. There's also a 1997 General Motors EV1 that survived the company's recall and subsequent destruction of the vehicles.

Ask the Man Who Owns One

The National Packard Museum opened in Warren, Ohio – the hometown of the Packard Brothers – in 1999. The 30-car collection covers the marque from its earliest days to its demise in the late 1950s. On display is the second oldest Packard in existence, a 1900 Model B. (To see the oldest Packard, head to Lehigh University in

Bethlehem, Pennsylvania where an 1899 Model A Roadster is on view in the lobby of the Packard Laboratory.)

The slickest car may well be a green-gold colored 1951 Packard Pan American convertible. At the 1952 New York International Motor Sports Show, #1 of this limited series won the top prize, the coveted Gold Trophy. The car here is #2 of the 6 Pan Americans that were built by Henney Motor Company.

A recent addition to the museum is the 1956 Packard Caribbean Convertible that Howard Hughes gave to his wife, the actress Jean Simmons. The car was donated by the Zimmerman Automobile Driving Museum in El Segundo, California. According to ADM co-founder Stanley Zimmerman, "The Board of the ADM wished that Packard lovers around the country have the opportunity to see this special car and most of them, at some time, will visit the National Packard Museum."

Packard's contribution to the war effort is represented by a 12-cylinder, 1,200 horsepower 4M 2500 Packard Marine Engine that was designed by Colonel Jesse Vincent. The engines were installed in groups of 3 or 4 in PT boats operating in the Pacific. The horsepower of each cylinder of the engine alone was more than their prewar Six engine.

Ask another man who owns one

Ohio has not one, but two, Packard museums. The other one is America's Packard Museum situated in a circa 1917 Packard dealership in the opposite end of the state in Dayton. Generally, around 50 cars are on view. A real speedster is the 1903 Model K Grey Wolf Racer that set a class record of 77.59 miles per hour on Ormond Beach. There are also two cars formerly owned by men named Al: Capone and Jolson. A highlight is the 1928 Vincent Speedster Model 626 prototype that Jesse Vincent designed and reached 129 mph in at the Packard Proving Grounds.

Coachbuilder Howard "Dutch" Darrin moved his coachbuilding operations to Los Angeles in 1937. He made his mark in the City of Angels by appealing to Hollywood stars, building the first of his "Packard Darrins" for actress Joan Blondell and later crafting cars for Clark Gable, Errol Flynn, and Carole Lombard. Packard built production versions of the custom bodied "Packard Darrins" in 1940 and 1941. The 1940 Model 120 convertible Victoria by Darrin that's on display was built from castings and molds by Dutch Darrin in 1971.

Crawford Auto-Aviation Museum at the Cleveland History Center 10825 East Boulevard, Cleveland, OH 44106

www.wrhs.org

National Packard Museum 1899 Mahoning Ave N.W., Warren, OH 44483

www.PackardMuseum.org

America's Packard Museum 420 S Ludlow Street, Dayton, OH 45402

www.AmericasPackardMuseum.org

Detroit Wheels: Exploring the Motor City's Automotive Heritage

Ford Piquette Avenue Plant Detroit, Michigan

Perhaps no other city in America has experienced the booming highs and sinking lows of Detroit. Many of those economic peaks and valleys are associated with the automotive industry of which the Motor City has heritage aplenty. But "Motown" is experiencing a renaissance; with a revitalized downtown and historic automotive sites getting some welcome TLC, there is much for a visitor to see.

Birthplace of the Model T

In 1904, when Henry Ford built his new manufacturing plant on Piquette Avenue, it would have been hard to predict that this humble brick building, modeled after a New England textile mill, would revolutionize the automotive industry, causing repercussions that were felt around the world. Ford developed the Model T on this site, and experimented with his assembly line method of production, which would ultimately reduce production time and cost. These two factors took cars, which up until then had been considered a rich person's plaything, and made them transportation for the masses.

The Ford Piquette Avenue Plant is now a museum with more than 70 vintage cars on display on two levels of the original production facility including the "Alphabet Collection," a sample of each of Ford's lettered models that were assembled both here and at its predecessor, the Mack Avenue Plant. Visitors will also see Henry Ford's recreated office (with a desk shrouded with blueprints, it's set up as if he just stepped onto the assembly line for a moment) along with the original "skunkworks," Ford's Experimental Room on the third floor, where he first conceived the Model T.

Twelve thousand Model Ts were assembled in this building. Ironically, for a vehicle that is so often associated with the color black, none of those built here were, in fact, black: the first six thousand were painted in Carmine Red. The oldest Model T in the collection is on display in the foyer, a 1909 Ford Model T Touring in red that's on loan; it sports serial number 220. Although the first year's output was designated as model year 1909, production had commenced in October 1908.

The oldest Ford here is a 1903 Model A Tonneau that was built at the Mack Avenue Plant. Dodge Brothers provided the chassis and two-speed transmission. The 1906 Ford Model N Runabout was the first car to be produced at the plant under mass production techniques and was an affordable ($600) bestseller.

One of Ford's breakthroughs was employing lightweight vanadium steel; enabling only two workers to lift a frame instead of four, making the production run more efficiently. Visitors can pick up a frame that's on display and marvel at how light it really is. They may also sit inside a 1915 Ford Model T Touring for a photo op.

Nestled among all the Brass Era motors, visitors can spot a real outlier: the 2004 Ford GT "Halo" car. Ford sought to make a marketing splash as it approached its centennial, and introduced this sporty pre-production vehicle, which reached 211.89 miles per hour on a track in Nardo, Italy.

Even without the cars, the Piquette Avenue Plant is a fascinating place to visit. The exposed wood columns encrusted with peeling paint, creaky wooden floors, and waist-to-ceiling windows that let in light and ventilation, are silent testament to the incredible automotive history that occurred in this space. The old line, "If these walls could talk," really rings true here.

Lions and Tigers and Cars, Oh My

The Detroit Historical Museum chronicles the history of Detroit from its founding to present day. While the exploits of the sports teams are amply covered, the museum houses an impressive collection devoted to Detroit's automotive heritage. The "America's Motor City" exhibit relays the story of automobile manufacturing and car culture in Detroit and features a "highlight car" that changes annually in late August thanks to local sponsors Warner Norcross + Judd. Recently it was a 1963 Chrysler Turbine that occupied pride-of-place at the entrance; it's one of less than a dozen remaining from Chrysler's 55-car experimental program. The aircraft-influenced body by Ghia is painted in a sleek color that can best be described as metallic pumpkin. Next up is a 1914 cyclecar; known as the "JB Rocket," built locally by the Scripps-Booth Cyclecar Company. Part car, part motorcycle, the body is so narrow that the two seats are configured one behind the other.

A two-story Cadillac "body drop" from the Clark Street assembly plant that closed in 1987 occupies pride-of-place in the center of the gallery. The operator had about sixty seconds to correctly drop the body onto the rolling chassis, a task they performed fifty times an hour. Visitors press a button to witness the body drop in action, then climb the stairs and watch the entire process from a viewing gallery up above. One area extols Detroit's "grease monkey" culture that led to many DIY car projects. Vintage tools and engine parts are on display here.

No other city in America has a richer automotive heritage than Detroit making it a must-see spot for car enthusiasts. In the words of Motown artist (and hometown gal) Martha Reeves, "Don't forget the Motor City."

Ford Piquette Avenue Plant 461 Piquette Avenue, Detroit, MI 48202

www.FordPiquettePlant.org

Detroit Historical Society 5401 Woodward Avenue, Detroit, MI 48202

www.DetroitHistorical.org

Iron City Classics

Frick Car and Carriage Museum Pittsburgh, Pennsylvania

If there were ever a car museum that is so pristine you could eat off the floor, it would likely be the Frick Car and Carriage Museum in Pittsburgh's East End. It's part of the much larger Frick Art & Historical Center, the legacy of Henry Clay Frick, a business magnate who at the height of the Gilded Age earned his coin in solid old-fashioned American industries like steel, railroads, and coal.

The museum, with its glowing white walls, ceiling, and clerestory windows, resembles a virtual reality set from *Logan's Run* more than a storage area for cars. It's a far cry from chimneys belching smoke at the local steel mill.

The focus here is on elegant horse-drawn carriages and vehicles from the early years of motoring, many of which were owned and used by the Frick family or produced in Western Pennsylvania. They relay the story of a time when cars were propelled by electricity, gas, and steam while car production was regional, creating some cars that are not seen elsewhere. During the 1990s the museum was expanded when local industrialist G. Whitney Snyder donated his automobile collection.

The earliest car in the collection is an 1898 Panhard et Levassor Tonneau. Howard Heinz, the son of the famous pickle magnate, initially brought it to Pittsburgh. It was an early pioneer, with the engine placed vertically at the front of the chassis, rather than under the seats or in the rear.

The 1903 Baker Electric Stanhope, with its smooth ride and handling, was known for comfort, and appealed to women. Because of cars like the Baker, electric charging stations were installed downtown, a feature that is reappearing more than a century later. In the alternative fuels category, steam power is represented by a fire-engine-red 1909 Stanley Model R Roadster that looks ready to take on all comers.

For all its leading heavy industry, it's surprising that Pittsburgh didn't become a center of the burgeoning automotive industry. One locally built car on display is the 1911 Penn Motor Company Penn 30 Touring Car. In fact, the Penn factory was only a few blocks from the museum. The Penn 30 was marketed as "the best at any price," which in this case was $1,075. The "30" in the name refers to the model's horsepower.

Another local legend is the 1917 Model E Touring Car produced by the Standard Steel Car Company. The builder of railroad cars entered the auto business in 1913, only to leave it a decade later.

An early racing car is the 1909 Keystone Six-Sixty Roadster produced in DuBois, Pennsylvania by the Munch-Allen Motor Car Company. The price was a whopping $2,250 for the six-cylinder, 60 horsepower speedster.

Normally there are about 24 vehicles on display, which rotate through from a larger collection. Although the model changes, there is always an American Bantam here; the cars were produced just north of Pittsburgh in the town of Butler. During a recent visit a red-and-blue 1939 Bantam Roadster, originally priced at $525, occupied pride of place near the front entrance. Its cartoonish size and appearance make sense as the Bantam is considered the inspiration for Donald Duck's car.

Adjacent to the car museum is Clayton, Frick's restored mansion, which is one of the few survivors along Pittsburgh's "Millionaire's Row." The art collection on display includes Renaissance-era paintings and other cultural delights, including vintage clothing and a greenhouse and gardens, to keep the non-car person in the family occupied. Admission to the Frick Art & Historical Center, including the Car and Carriage Museum, is free.

Frick Car and Carriage Museum 7227 Reynolds Street, Pittsburgh, PA 15208
www.TheFrickPittsburgh.org

SEE MORE AT THE GILMORE

GILMORE CAR MUSEUM Hickory Corners, Michigan

Saying the Gilmore Car Museum is just another car museum is like saying the Mona Lisa is just another painting.

A trip to the 400-vehicle Gilmore in Hickory Corners, Michigan is really like visiting more than a half-dozen car museums at one time, each of which could be a destination all by itself. Coming across it in the rolling farmland of southwest Michigan is like discovering an automotive Shangri-La. Their tagline is "Telling the History of America Through the Automobile" and, somehow, they manage to pull off that enormous task.

Included at the sight are separate buildings housing partner museums including the Lincoln Motor Car Heritage Museum, Cadillac-LaSalle Club Museum and Research Center, Classic Car

Club of America Museum, Model A Ford Museum, Pierce-Arrow Museum, H. H. Franklin Club Museum, Museum of the Horseless Carriage, a motorcycle collection, recreated 1930s Shell service station, toy cars, automotive mascots, eight restored 19th-century barns and more. Did I mention they also have a Tucker? You could easily spend multiple days here.

The seeds of the museum were planted in 1963 when Donald Gilmore, who had retired as head of pharmaceutical company Upjohn, had a lot of time on his hands. His wife, Genevieve, gave him a 1920 Pierce-Arrow to restore and that's when it all began. (Can we all just agree on how cool Genevieve was?) As is often the case with car collecting, you can't stop with just one and the 400 plus vehicle collection stands as a testament to the Gilmore's perseverance as collectors.

Before becoming overwhelmed, it's best to start out in the main building, also known as the Gilmore Heritage Center. This is where themed temporary exhibits, like Greatest Generation: The Evolution of America's Sports Cars, are displayed. Rarities include a 1963 Chrysler Turbine which, with its jet inspired turbine engine, was the car of the future, until it wasn't. Fifty were farmed out to motorists around the country for three-month test drives.

A 1948 Tucker #1047 in Waltz Blue is another showstopper. Made famous in the popular zeitgeist by the 1988 Francis Ford Coppola film *Tucker: The Man and His Dream*, only 51 of the streamlined cars were produced and this is one of the 47 survivors. As one of the last Tuckers built, it had only eight miles on the odometer when it was acquired by the museum.

A sampling of the permanent exhibits includes: Born to Perform – The Era of The Muscle Car that highlights what, for many classic car buffs, is the golden age of automobile production; The Negro Motorist Green Book, the guidebook produced by Victor Green that, in the Jim Crow era, directed African Americans to restaurants, lodging and other businesses that would welcome them; and Toy Cars of Yesteryear, featuring more than 150 post World War II tin toy cars include rarities produced in occupied Germany and Japan.

Four of the museums – Cadillac LaSalle Club, Lincoln Motor Car Heritage, H.H. Franklin Collection and the Model A Ford Museum – were built to look like vintage car dealerships.

The Cadillac LaSalle Club building represents the sleek lines of a dealership that had been designed by GM in 1948. Inside, Cadillacs and LaSalles from 1903 to the 21st century are on display in a virtual time warp for a customer seeking a new luxury automobile. Remember the 1993 Cadillac Allanté Roadster? Bodies were produced by Pininfarina in Turin, Italy then shipped to America on specially equipped 747s. This is one of 30 pace cars that were produced for the Indy Festival Parade for the 1992 Indy 500 race and is signed by that year's winner, Al Unser, Jr.

2022 marks the 100th anniversary of the acquisition of The Lincoln Motor Company by Henry Ford. On display are 30 varieties from this luxury marque including a 1922 Lincoln Sport Phaeton, a 1937 Lincoln-Zephyr coupe that looks like it jumped off the screen from *Who Framed Roger Rabbit?* and an elegant 1956 Lincoln Continental Mark II sport coupe.

From 1902 through 1934 the H.H. Franklin Manufacturing Company of Syracuse, NY was building cars powered by innovative air-cooled engines. Not many survived so it's a rarity to find them in museums. Other than the Franklin Automobile Museum in Tucson, Arizona, this is the biggest assemblage of Franklins I've seen in one place. Because the air-cooling removed the need for a bulky radiator upfront, Franklins front ends took on some interesting shapes including horse collars, shovels, and barrel hoods. A 1916 Franklin advertisement in the exhibit noted that Franklin Direct Air-Cooling eliminated 177 parts which meant lighter weight, greater efficiency, and lower maintenance.

In the Ford Model A Museum, a 1928 Ford Model A is the first second generation Model A produced. It was given to Ford's friend Thomas Edison who asked that the body be changed from a Tudor to a Phaeton.

The Gilmore is so big that there's even a museum devoted to automotive mascots and hood ornaments. The breadth of motifs

– from sultry figures to spaceships to Egyptian sphinxes – is astonishing.

It's not all just looking at cars and objects. The Gilmore has a busy activity schedule for hands-on experiences. The very popular Model T Driving Experience teaches motorists the complicated process of cruising along in a vintage Ford Model T; it was operated with three foot pedals, one hand lever and two controls on the steering wheel. During the Ride the Classics program from May through September visitors hop aboard for a jaunt in cars from the collection. Past rides have included a 1931 Ford Model Woody Wagon, 1935 Austin London Taxi, and a 1963 Cadillac convertible.

Since you'll be here for hours, or even days, there are places to eat on the museum campus. I can attest to the locally made blueberry pie at George & Sally's Blue Moon Diner as a satisfying pick me up. The 1941 Silk Diner was moved here from Meriden, Connecticut.

While the museum is open year-round, note that some of the individual museums and collections on-site are closed from December through March. Go to the website for more detailed information. Here you'll also find out the dates for themed car shows including Corvette Envy, DeutscheMarques and more.

Gilmore Car Museum 6865 Hickory Road, Hickory Corners, MI 49060
GilmoreCarMuseum.org

FORDS AND MORE

HENRY FORD MUSEUM OF AMERICAN INNOVATION Dearborn, MI

The Henry Ford Museum (known locally just as "the Henry Ford") in the Detroit suburb of Dearborn is one of the greatest assemblages of American history. Henry Ford was a known collector in Americana and, since he had unlimited funds, left no stone unturned in acquiring highlights of American heritage.

The museum is divided into two main segments: the Henry Ford Museum of American Innovation and Greenfield Village.

The former focuses on exhibits devoted to automobiles, aviation, manufacturing, housing, the fight for freedom, railroads, clocks, jewelry, mathematics and more.

Greenfield Village is a collection of historic structures including Thomas Edison's laboratory, the Wright Brothers' workshop and more. Exhibits are also devoted to the ingenuity of Henry Ford. You can even take a ride in a Model T.

The scope of the museum is so large that it can't be covered in one article, so I'll focus on a few unusual vehicles at the core of the collection, the "Driving America" exhibit.

Perhaps no American car has had as big a debut as the 1964 ½ Ford Mustang. Henry Ford II officially unveiled the Mustang on April 17, 1964, in the Ford Pavilion at the World's Fair in New York. That same day the car was available at Ford dealers across the country as a media blitz blanketed all three TV networks, newspapers, and TV Guide with ads for the new sporty vehicle.

The museum has not one, but two, unique Mustangs in house. The first is a Wimbledon White 1965 Mustang convertible with serial #1, or to be more precise 5F08F100001. A St. John's, Newfoundland airline pilot named Stanley Tucker (what a great car name!) purchased it from local dealer Parsons Ford three days before the public was supposed to get their hands on one. Realizing the importance of the car, Ford tried to buy it back from the pilot but was rebuffed. Finally, in 1966, they offered him a trade of the one millionth Mustang, fully loaded, and he accepted.

Another Mustang (although more in name and spirit) here is the 1962 Mustang I Roadster concept car. Dan Gurney ran the mid-engine car in demonstration laps at Watkins Glen and Laguna Seca. (It was just Mustang at the time, the "I" designation came later.) With its aerodynamic headlights, long nose and rear quarter panel side scoops, honk if you think it resembles the Ford GT that arrived four decades later. While the car didn't become the Mustang pony car that eventually hit the scene, the halo effect of the design (and the name) had to have played on buyer's minds.

Other highlights of the "Driving America" exhibit include: the 1896 Ford Quadricycle Runabout that was the first car built by Henry Ford; a 1931 Bugatti Royale Type 41 convertible; a 1937 Cord 812 convertible; 1948 Tucker #1016 – naturally, it's black; and a 2016 General Motors first-generation self-driving test car. The 1865 Roper steam carriage is considered the oldest surviving American made car.

It's not all chrome and glitz though. The 1984 Plymouth Voyager

Minivan is on display because this is, first and foremost, a history museum. And Lee Iacocca's creation changed the face of suburban life. It might not be pretty, but the minivan is certainly historic.

The 1974 Warrior concept car on display has a unique story behind it. In 1953 its creator, McKinley Thompson, Jr., won a *Motor Trend* automotive design contest and was eventually hired by Ford as the first African American designer with the company. During World War II he served in the US Army Signal Corps and likely had direct experience with amphibious vehicles.

Thompson helped create the designs of the Mustang, GT40, Thunderbird and Bronco. After retiring from Ford, he used a Renault 10 chassis to build an all-purpose vehicle called the Warrior, envisioning the inexpensive lightweight dune-buggy-style vehicle with a one-piece floating fiberglass body as a transportation solution for Third World countries.

With a freeboard of 10 inches, Thompson claimed that the Warrior's tires could propel it along at 2 knots. The front wheels also produced enough of a rudder effect for in-water steering. According to Curator of Transportation Matt Anderson, "The Warrior has a lot of presence on the museum floor. Visitors can't walk by it without stopping for a closer look."

Vintage neon signs from businesses like McDonald's and Holiday Inn complete the Driving America tableau.

Don't miss the Ford Rouge factory tour to see F-150 pickup trucks being assembled. At one time the factory was a behemoth, with more than 100,000 workers. Today there about 6,000 but it's still an impressive facility. You'll start out with an immersive movie about the manufacturing process then the highlight of the tour: strolling on a catwalk above the production line. Check ahead to see if there is production scheduled on the day of your visit.

There is so much to see and do so if you come to the Henry Ford, plan on spending several days here.

Henry Ford Museum of American Innovation 20900 Oakwood Boulevard, Dearborn, MI 48124 www.TheHenryFord.org

Upscale "Barn Finds" on Cape Cod

HERITAGE MUSEUMS AND GARDENS Sandwich, Massachusetts

The Heritage Museums and Gardens in Sandwich, Massachusetts – with a car museum, vintage carousel, acres of gardens, and American folk-art galleries – has something for everyone, which is a good thing: you get to explore the cars to your hearts content while others in your group can pursue their own interests.

I've visited so many car museums that I don't always say "wow" at first when I see one, but this one boasts the wow factor. The 40-car collection is housed in a bucolic setting on New England's Cape Cod: a re-creation of the stone round barn found at Hancock Shaker Village in Pittsfield, Massachusetts. The original dates to 1826; this replica was built in 1969 by the museum's founder, Josiah K. Lilly III, a scion of the famed pharmaceutical family.

Lilly started collecting cars in 1964 with the purchase of a 1916 Simplex Crane Model 5 Touring. He preferred early American automobiles – the collection is rich in the pre-World War II era. Lilly enjoyed the camaraderie of the classic car community, so he decided to share his collection with the public. With room for about two dozen vehicles in the two-level barn, not all the cars are on display at one time. Fortunately, the museum makes its overflow on view with a glass-fronted storage area.

The 1909 White Steam Car is #9 on the National Historic Vehicle Register. The original owner, President William Howard Taft, used it as a limousine and it was the first car to be owned by a US president. Taft was such an advocate of the automobile he converted the White House stables into a garage. He also chose this model over a Stanley Steamer, preferring the White's technologically advanced steam recycling system. However, technology came at a price: the White Steam Car cost four times more than the 1911 Stanley Steamer Model 62 Runabout that is also in the museum's collection.

The 1916 Brewster is completely original down to its leather fenders and wicker exterior, which sort of makes it look like a giant picnic basket on wheels. The company was known for making custom automobiles for wealthy clients; hence the reason this model included a speaking tube, making it easier for the owner to bellow out orders to the chauffeur from the back seat. It's a nice touch, back seat drivers today just scream in your ear.

This backseat driver problem was eliminated in the 1903 Stevens-Duryea Runabout Model L – the driver actually sat in the back. The car was easily started with a short crank attached to the steering column.

When Josiah Lilly started collecting, the "3Ps of Motordom" were highly desirable. Examples from this alphabetic trio here include: a 1910 Peerless Model 27 Roadster, 1912 Packard 1-48 Victoria, and a 1919 Pierce-Arrow. A century later, these cars still impress.

While a 1922 Ford Model T is not rare, the one on display here is: it was modified by the Howe Fire Apparatus Company to be a pumper. This is a rare fire engine that was built on a Model T car chassis rather than a truck chassis.

Buyers in the early 1930s had the opportunity to purchase cars at separate ends of the pricing spectrum. An affordable 1932 Auburn Boattail Speedster costing $975 ($16,000 in today's dollars) is a sharp contrast in price, size and styling compared to an estimated $14,000 ($230,000 today) for the 1930 Duesenberg Model J Derham Tourster. The latter once belonged to actor Gary Cooper; at that price, it's not surprising only 8 were built. (The chassis alone was $9,500.)

The Heritage Museums and Gardens are open seasonally from mid-April through mid-October. Please note that some of the cars rotate from the main exhibition space to storage. However, in-depth curator led "Behind-the-Scenes Auto Storage Tours" are offered twice a month.

Heritage Museums & Gardens 67 Grove Street, Sandwich, MA 02563
www.HeritageMuseumsAndGardens.org

Keep on Trucking (and Tractoring) in Virginia

Keystone Truck & Tractor Museum Colonial Heights, Virginia

There's something for everyone at the sprawling Keystone Truck & Tractor Museum in Colonial Heights, Virginia. Despite its name, in addition to the 185 tractors and 100 trucks, there are about two dozen classic cars along with ten fire engines and a handful of motorcycles, scooters and bicycles.

The collection is rounded out with 2,000 toy trucks plus Petroliana and Americana that includes antique gas pumps, vintage tools, tobacco farming memorabilia and a treeful of chainsaws.

The museum is the result of the collecting passion of Keith Jones, who started out with his four brothers in the no-stoplight town of Abilene, Virginia. His dad operated a sawmill so by his teen years he was hauling lumber and working at the family's filling station.

The Jones siblings went on to found trucking company Abilene Motor Express, which they sold a few years ago.

I've visited the Keystone Truck & Tractor Museum several times over the past few years and am amazed to see that each time the museum has grown larger, and sure enough, at 120,000 square feet in 2021 it's even bigger still. Jones bought his first tractor – a 1950 John Deere M – in 1997 from his late uncle's estate, which he then ended up restoring, and says that's when he got the "collecting fever." He's still running hot as he keeps acquiring new vehicles and sharing them with the public.

Jones opened the museum in 2010. Until then his collection was stored in trailers. He recalls, "We thought we'd need about half the space we have here. The collection is growing, so we might have to do some rearranging."

One of the most popular acquisitions is a veritable time capsule that sits out front attracting traffic whizzing by on I-95: a vintage 1951 car hauler with four 1956 Chevys perched on top. When Jones found it, the trailer had been sitting outside for 40 years.

The first impression as visitors venture inside the museum is the row upon row of tractors in various shades of green (John Deere, Waterloo, Oliver, Case, Massey-Harris), amber (Minneapolis-Moline, Allis-Chalmers) and red (McCormick, Moline, Farmall, Cockshutt, International Harvester, Graham-Bradley, Thieman) making a birds-eye view of the display floor look like a colossal traffic signal wrought in farming equipment. The passel of Fordson tractors in battleship gray set off to the side look out of place in this polychromatic array.

The 1932 Massey-Harris GP with a 25-horsepower L head Hercules engine boasted a revolutionary feature, it was a tractoring pioneer with the first four-wheel drive but, despite this technological advance, it still had a hand cranked starter.

With its hump on the body, a 1959 Massey-Ferguson 65 looks a bit like a camel. The hump hides the LPG tank that was more popular on tractors down south. The 1949 McCormick O-4 has a streamlined appearance due to its role as an orchard tractor – to prevent getting clogged in fruit tree branches there are metal skirts over the wheels and cowlings over the fuel caps.

One of the most popular tractors is the 1938 Minneapolis-Moline UDLX. It boasts a car-like appearance, with an enclosed cab and amenities including a radio, heater, and clock. The slogan was "farm during the day, drive to town at night." Hard to believe with all that bling it wasn't a sales success. But there was still a Depression going on and according to my museum guide, "It was too expensive, and farmers thought you were a wuss if you had a cab on your tractor."

Another 1938 is a Graham Bradley Standard Model 104 built by Graham-Paige. With its swept back nose and stylish side louvered panels it looked ready to race. It became known as a "rich man's" tractor and enjoyed an all too brief history. They were sold exclusively through Sears Roebuck but were removed from the catalog by 1940.

The 1918 Moline Universal Tractor is referred to as the first row-crop tractor. The standard equipment of electric lights, rheostat throttle and electric starter were quite advanced for that period.

Despite their popularity with the public, museum curator Alan "Bones" Stone is not a big fan of the Deere tractors. Decades of working on and meticulously restoring tractors have taught him that the parts aren't interchangeable between Deeres, often even among the same year, unlike they are on other makes such as International Harvester and Fordson. "Deere is a triumph of marketing," he says. "Every little kid has a John Deere toy so that's the brand they grow up knowing."

The museum purchased a container of tractors from Europe which included a few marques more known for sports cars, including a 1957 Porsche P111, which was licensed by Mannesmann AG, and a 1962 Lamborghini Model 1R.

The mammoth German-built 1939 Lanz Bulldog single cylinder hot-bulb semi-diesel engine has one of the more archaic starting systems. It's a 20-minute process that involves a blowtorch, along with the driver taking the steering wheel and shaft out of the cabin and inserting it into the side of the engine to crank it up. It's not exactly conducive to quick startups.

Although Jones' first love was tractors, he is a trucking guy, so there's a wide variety of trucks to choose from including a 1936 IH C-30 4x2, 1939 Mack BM in Yellow Transit Co. livery hauling a 25,000-pound payload 1935 Fruehauf trailer, 1945 Dodge WH 47 tanker, 1954 Autocar DC-75, and a 1973 Chevrolet 90 6x4.

One of the great independent truck makers out of Detroit was the Federal Motor Truck Company. They produced the 1941 Federal Model 24 4x2 that was operated by the American Thermos Bottle Company of Norwich, Connecticut.

A real rarity is the 1957 Diamond T "Pig Nose Truck," so named because the owner wanted more power and added an extra engine to the front, giving it the appearance of a porcine snout.

The handful of campers include perhaps the coolest camper of all, a 1969 Diamond REO HD275 Trend chassis with a cab made from Royalex fiberglass hauling a 22' Country Wagon camper. Since the camper is on the elevated flatbed of a truck, you'll need a stepladder to climb inside, but you'll be the king of any KOA campground in this behemoth.

Classic cars are not left out and focus mainly on 1950s brands and 1960s muscle cars including a stable of 1955-56-57 Ford Thunderbirds and a 1967 Chevrolet Chevelle Custom hot rod.

There is also a popular casual restaurant on site for down home southern diner food.

Keystone Truck & Tractor Museum 880 W Roslyn Road, Colonial Heights, VA 23834
www.KeystoneTractorWorks.com

Spotlight on Military Vehicles

National Museum of the US Army Fort Belvoir, Virginia

It's hard to believe but, until now, the United States Army, the oldest branch of America's armed forces, had no official museum dedicated to its complete heritage. That oversight has now been corrected. In 2020, 245 years after the United States Army's birth in 1775 as a colonial militia, the National Museum of the United States Army opened in Fort Belvoir, Virginia, about 20 miles southwest of Washington, DC.

Despite years of planning, it was a bumpy road to get here. The museum's original opening date in April 2020 was pushed back due to Covid. However, on 11 November, Veteran's Day in the United States, the mission was completed as a gala opening took place.

Commanding an 84-acre site, the 185,500 square foot building contains 11 galleries – arranged chronologically from founding the nation in the 18th century, to operations in today's changing world – and 1,400 artifacts to tell the story of the US Army through its impact on the individual soldier.

Highlights of the collection include a sword and scabbard wielded by Captain John Berry, commander of the Water Battery at Fort McHenry while it was under British bombardment during the War of 1812; a Civil War 12-pounder "Napoleon" cannon; and an M1 Garand Rifle carried by paratrooper Private Martin J. Teahan as he parachuted into Normandy on D-Day. He was later killed along with more than half the men of the 508th Infantry Regiment.

In addition to smaller artifacts, the museum spotlights about a dozen vehicles operated on water (D-Day Landing Craft, Vehicle, Personnel LCVP Higgins Boat), land (M4A3E2 Sherman Tank that fought in the Battle of the Bulge), and air (Vietnam War Hu-1 Huey Helicopter).

The oldest "vehicle" here is a pedestrian mule. The army starting using this hybrid of a horse and a donkey as a pack animal in the mid 19th-century. Using less food and forage than a horse, mules could haul an average of 400 pounds. They became so beloved within the ranks that it in 1899 the United States Military Academy at West Point football team adopted the mule as its mascot.

Move forward in time to a World War I-era Renault FT-17 Light Tank that was assigned to Company C, 344th Tank Battalion, American Expeditionary Forces (AEF) Tank Brigade, under a young Lt. Col. George S. Patton, Jr. The company saw action in the St. Mihiel Salient and the Toul, before participating in the Meuse-Argonne Offensive. It was nicknamed the "Five of Hearts" after the insignia painted on the turret. The "Five of Hearts" was sent to Fort Meade, Maryland, in 1919 and transferred to the museum almost a century later.

The 7-ton Renault featured a four-cylinder, 35 hp motor with a top speed of 5 mph and a range of 22 miles. The example on view is the only documented surviving FT-17 tank operated by U.S. forces in World War I. Its revolutionary design – including a fully rotating turret – was used by the U.S. Army as the basis for America's first tank, the Model 1917.

By 1917 the army needed to standardize its haphazard fleet of motor vehicles and developed the three-ton cargo truck known as the Standard B Liberty Truck, a vehicle with interchangeable parts to simplify field maintenance. The three-ton Liberty Truck showcased was built in 1918 and offered a 52 hp gasoline engine that propelled it to a top speed of 15 mph.

Few Liberty Trucks made it overseas for World War I, but the truck took on added historical significance when the army sent a transcontinental motor convoy across America in 1919. The 81-vehicle, 3,251-mile journey, which included Liberty Trucks, was designed to test army mobility in wartime conditions. Lt. Col. Dwight Eisenhower was part of the slow-moving caravan and realized that American roads were in shoddy condition. That, and his exposure to the modern German autobahn during World War II, influenced his decision, as president, to authorize the nation's interstate highway system.

The M4 Sherman tank was deployed to all theaters in World War II. In 1944 the army produced the M4A3E2 Sherman tank like the "Cobra King" on display. On 26 December 1944, the Cobra King spearheaded the 4th Armored Division column that broke through the German line at the Battle of the Bulge, then met its ultimate demise in an unsuccessful effort to liberate American POWs near Hammelburg, Germany in March 1945. Fitted with thick frontal armor and a larger turret to support a 75-mm main gun, it tipped the scale at 33 tons.

There is physical evidence showing that the Cobra King experienced a brief internal fire and explosions that damaged the tank's interior on this mission. It was abandoned after the raid with its location unknown. After performing a great deal of research, Army Chaplain Keith Goode found the "First in Bastogne" tank on display in Germany in 2004. In 2009, the U.S. Army Center of Military History shipped Cobra King back to the U.S. for restoration.

For road warriors the most interesting vehicle may be the High Mobility Multipurpose Wheeled Vehicle (HMMWV). Deployed by the thousands in the desert terrains of Afghanistan and Iraq, the Humvee on view here is like no other, it's the first production Humvee assembled in January 1985 and is serial number 000001.

The Humvee was the product of the army's 1981 Program XM998 to develop a light, tactical four-wheel drive utility vehicle. AM General bested Chrysler Defense and Teledyne Continental to win the competition. Based in Indiana, AM General's lineage includes Willys-Overland Motors, a producer of jeeps during World War II.

On their initial deployment in Iraq Humvees were infamous for being under-armored and didn't offer solid protection against enemy fire. An exhibit reveals what troops in the field did to upgrade their vehicles with parts on hand. Scrap metal was cut up and welded to up-armor the vehicle in a device known, somewhat facetiously, as a "Hillbilly Door." Eventually the army grasped this need and provided Armor Survivability Kits featuring armor plate and ballistic glass windows.

In the Changing World Gallery, one of the heftiest objects is the battle-scarred M3 Bradley Cavalry Fighting Vehicle that was assigned to A Troop, 3rd Squadron, 7th Cavalry, known as the Apaches. It was the lead vehicle in the 2003 charge from Kuwait to Baghdad and helped secure Baghdad International Airport.

Sometimes the army must reluctantly get its feet wet. A nautical transport showcased is the 1942 LCVP (Landing Craft, Vehicle, Personnel), or Higgins boat, one of the few surviving landing craft that was used in the D-Day landings in Normandy. It was found on the Isle of Wight by Overlord Research and transported to Danville, Virginia for restoration. The plywood hulled boats, capable of 12 knots, carried 36 combat-loaded troops or one jeep and 12 men.

The smallest vehicle is about the size of the BB8 droid in Star Wars, and probably just as nimble over rough terrain. The prototype for the Multi-Function Agile Radio-Controlled Robot (MARCbot) was designed in the field using parts from commercial components, which probably explains why it looks so similar to a remote-controlled car an eager child would unwrap under the Christmas tree. The lightweight mobile device was first deployed in Iraq to inspect suspicious objects such as IEDs. The camera attached to its mobile arm could peer behind doors and around obstacles.

The MARCbot is parked next to a speedier ride, a flashy Honda CG125 commuter motorcycle that was captured from a Taliban fighter in Zabul Province, Afghanistan in 2010. Powered by a 124 cc, four-stroke OV engine, they've been produced in Pakistan since 1992 by Atlas Honda Ltd.

While the focus for this story has been vehicles, they take up a small portion of the exhibits. For anyone interested in a comprehensive look at the history of the United States Army over the centuries, the museum is a must-visit attraction.

National Museum of the United States Army 1775 Liberty Drive, Fort Belvoir, VA 22060

www.thenmusa.org

The Real Philly Special

SIMEONE FOUNDATION AUTOMOTIVE MUSEUM
Philadelphia, Pennsylvania

Cities often tout their world-class amenities, and Philadelphia certainly has its share. But beyond historic and cultural treasures, such as Independence Hall and the Museum of Art, another world caliber attraction is hiding in plain sight near the Philadelphia International Airport: The Simeone Foundation Automotive Museum.

"The Simeone," as it's known colloquially, is a unique collection of 75 race cars of historical significance that has earned it accolades from around the globe. Founded by Dr. Fred Simeone, a retired Philadelphia neurosurgeon, the museum has twice been honored (in 2011 and again in 2017) as Museum of the Year by *Octane* magazine, the renowned British automotive journal.

Simeone has a knack for appearing on the top of lists. In 2019, he was ranked the number-one classic car collector in the world by The Key, an annual list compiled by the prestigious Liechtenstein-based Classic Car Trust, due to the quality of his car collection, the exposure of the cars to the public and the museum's educational mission, including its extensive research library which is among the world's largest automotive-themed libraries. It includes more than a century's worth of periodicals, photographs, and sales literature for review (by prior request) by historians and car restorers.

Letting the public access the collection is key, if you will, which helped vault Simeone past such famous collectors as Ralph Lauren and Jay Leno. According to Simeone, "I think it's important that the public can see the cars. You know I gave these away to the foundation. When I'm gone the collection will still be open." *(Note: Dr. Simeone passed away in 2022 but, just as he planned, his museum will live on.)*

The collection is housed in a former engine remanufacturing facility in southwest Philadelphia, tucked away behind car dealerships and body shops. The nondescript location belies the interior, where cars are set out in realistic dioramic tableaux representing the historic circuits they raced, including Daytona, Watkins Glen, and the Targa Florio. Visitors can practically smell the oily exhaust and hear the rumble of the revving engines, transported back to a time can when drivers raced in open cockpit cars wearing goggles and leather helmets to protect them from muddy tracks.

The quality of historic cars at the Simeone is second to none. The most prominent in the collection is the 1964 Shelby Cobra Daytona Coupe CSX 2287, the prototype racing coupe is one of the most important cars created by automotive legend Carroll Shelby. It achieved 23 land speed records at Utah's Bonneville Salt Flats and was the first car named to the National Historic Vehicle Register by the US-based Historic Vehicle Association.

According to Simeone, who grew up in Philly admiring cars, "The entrance exam for a car to get in here is pretty tough. Every automobile here has a compelling story, which is very important.

All these cars had great drivers, great stories and then made their mark in history by winning races."

This Philadelphia story begins in the hardscrabble neighborhood of Kensington (also home to cinematic boxer Rocky Balboa) with a tale of a father passing along his love of cars to his son, an important lesson as the hobby tries to appeal to the next generation.

According to Simeone, "I'd say that my love of cars was 100% passed down from my father, but I think he wanted to keep me off the road. He found an old 1949 Alfa for me that was all beat up. I had to put it back together to drive it. Some of his cars are in the collection including the 1921 Duesenberg 183 Grand Prix Race Car, 1937 Cord 812 Supercharged, 1935 Auburn 851 Boattail Speedster, and a 1956 Mercedes-Benz 300SL Gullwing Coupe that he found on a used car lot. It still has its original paint and upholstery."

Originality is important to Simeone as he is a believer in preservation versus restoration, "If a car has its original features, even if it's not perfect, you want to leave it that way. Because once you start stripping it and changing it the car bears little resemblance to how it left the factory and then it becomes your creation rather than the creation of the manufacturer."

That 1921 Duesenberg is a premier example of a barn find, in this case in one of the most unlikely places. Simeone continues, "I grew up in a poor part of Philadelphia and the Duesenberg was inside a garage there in pieces when my dad bought it for almost nothing. It turns out to have been one of the 1921 French Grand Prix race cars, the only race before World War II that an American car won overseas."

The 1907 Renault Racing Roadster is one that automotive pioneer William K. Vanderbilt II raced on Long Island. Other owners of this model included names like Whitney and Guggenheim, pointing to the exclusivity of this early French car.

Simeone set up the cars in context of where they achieved fame. He says, "When you think of the GT40 you think of Le Mans, when you think of our Daytona Cobra Coupe you think of Bonneville because that's where it set 23 records. So, we've placed the cars in those settings."

The "America at Le Mans" exhibit features a 1927 Stutz AA Blackhawk Challenger, 1929 Stutz Model M Supercharged (with a body designed by Stutz employee Gordon Beurig), 1929 duPont Model G Le Mans Speedster, 1966 Ford GT40 MKII and a 1967 Ford GT40 MK IV.

He has a special for fondness for Brooklands. "People could join the club at Brooklands to race their cars on its steep oval track. How did they even have the guts to build that in 1908? It was Brooklands that saved the sports car for England and probably the rest of the world."

Simeone designed the dioramas and put them together with props he found on Craigslist. The Brooklands diorama is so lifelike that when I posted a photo of the 1933 Alfa Romeo 8C 2300 Spider parked in the display on social media a while back someone kept insisting to me that the photo was taken at the actual Brooklands.

As for his favorite it's difficult to choose, but Simeone leans towards the flame-red 1938 Alfa Romeo 8C 2900B MM Spyder. It occupies a place of honor on a spinning turntable: its sultry curves are pure rolling sculpture, cloaking a powerplant that won the prestigious 1938 Mille Miglia open road endurance race in northern Italy. A close second for Simeone is the 1952 Cunningham C-4R Roadster that won its class at Le Mans in 1954, the first American-manufactured car to do so.

The cars here are not meant to just be admired behind velvet ropes. The museum is a popular destination on bi-weekly Demo Days, when select vehicles are taken out on the back lot for a rumbling drive.

"It's important for people to see, hear and even smell these remarkable machines," says Simeone. The growl of vintage engines mingles with the roar of airplanes overhead in their take off pattern at PHL, providing a wonderful afternoon outing for hundreds of gearheads.

Until then, the museum's website at www.SimeoneMuseum.org can keep one busy for hours with detailed stories and videos about the cars.

In an era of Uber and self-driving cars, Simeone is also focused on generating interest among the next generation of potential car fans. He says, "Our long-term plan is to keep developing the museum's theme of 'The Spirit of Competition' and continue our new programs that are geared towards the education of youngsters. The focus in schools now is on STEM (science, technology, engineering, and mathematics). We add "arts" because automobile design includes that aspect."

The museum runs STEAM summer camps for children aged 6 to 15, designed to make learning fun and practical. One activity has campers designing and building cars out of blocks of wood, then testing their aerodynamics in a smoke chamber wind tunnel and see how it compares to the 1964 Shelby Daytona Cobra. According to Simeone, "The long-term plan when I am gone is to keep developing our new programs that are geared towards the education of youngsters."

Fred Simeone created a museum and resource in Philadelphia that will continue to inspire and benefit the next generation of automotive enthusiasts. That's quite a world-class legacy.

Simeone Foundation Automotive Museum 6825 Norwitch Drive, Philadelphia, PA 19153
www.SimeoneMuseum.org

Automotive innovations in Florida

Tampa Bay Automobile Museum Tampa Bay, Florida

Most car museums focus on the sleek lines of classic automobiles: visitors swoon over pointed tail fins, curvaceous fenders, and glossy colors. It takes an engineer, however, to see beyond the beauty and focus on what's under the hood: the prop shafts, and pistons, and chassis that make each car different.

One such engineer is French-born Alain Cerf. With a background in mechanical engineering, he founded Polypack, a global packaging equipment manufacturer and designer. Cerf's particular interest in automotive technology is on full display at his "side project," also known as the Tampa Bay Automobile Museum – a collection of more than 65 vehicles on Florida's Gulf Coast.

Cerf, along with his son Olivier, has compiled a world-class automotive collection that highlights innovation over the years and the engineers and designers responsible for them. As Alain says, "Sometimes innovation works, and sometimes it doesn't. I like to showcase the engineers who make it possible."

He has a soft spot for vehicles designed in the 1920s and 1930s, particularly those with front-wheel drive and rear engines. But despite all the focus on engineering, the cars are also beautiful; some of the vehicles like the Tatras, possess fluid lines that are also rolling works of art.

As impressive as the collection is, at one time some of them were merely "used" cars. Alain recalls, "When I was young, I was not collecting classic cars, but buying cheap cars like a Delahaye, Talbot or Salmson, which were not considered collectible yet. The first one was a Peugeot Darl'mat, which is still running as good as the other ones."

A section of British motoring might is led off by the 1953 prototype of the Jensen 541, which entered production the following year. Designed by Eric Neale, Cerf considers it to be the best-looking car to come out of the West Bromwich factory. Not content to rest on its good looks, it was also a superbly aerodynamic vehicle with a drag coefficient of just 0.39, one of the lowest recorded at the time. The rare auto on display here is the actual Jensen prototype that was built for the Earl's Court Motor Show in London.

The 1950 Allard P1 is representative of the first British racecar to win the Rallye Monte Carlo after a long absence. Sidney Allard himself and Guy Warburton drove it to victory. Its Ford V-8 engine made repairs easier for the export market in the US.

The 1965 Ford Mustang was shipped across the pond to Great Britain to be converted into an all-wheel drive vehicle by Ferguson Research. Although it drove well, Ford was not convinced that the successful pony car needed this modification in widespread production.

The 1929 Ruxton prototype, with its distinctive cat's-eye headlights, was the first attempt at a front-wheel drive vehicle in the United States. Except for a few other cars like the Cord, the concept didn't really catch on and wasn't resurrected again in the US until the 1966 on a Toronado. And that's how Cerf rolls. His collection seeks out automotive innovations, some of which were quite unusual that faded away, and others of which eventually made it into mainstream production.

An example of the former is an area dedicated to the sleeve valve engine – also known as the "Silent Knight – a technology developed in America by Charles Yale Knight that disappeared in 1939. Three examples on display are a 1928 Willys-Knight Type 56, a 1927 Avions Voisin, and a 1939 Panhard Dynamic.

Cerf has an affinity for Czech-built Tatras, with seven in the collection. The 1930 Tatra T26/30 Open Tourer took a roundabout route to Florida. The sturdy military vehicle was purchased by a representative of Studebaker in the US to learn more about its technology, including a central tube chassis and aluminum, air-cooled boxer engine. It was discovered in a crate emblazoned with "Studebaker" in Ohio. Despite traveling all that distance, it still has less than 5,000 original miles.

The rear-engine 1942 Tatra T 87 was produced in Czechoslovakia. One of its distinctive features is the central tail fin affixed to the back, creating a shark-like appearance. Hungarian Paul Jaray designed the all-steel body; he is also known for the aerodynamic styling of early airships that led to the Zeppelin's familiar streamlined presence in the sky. Several years before the vaunted debut of the Tucker, the Tatra had already offered three headlights in front.

The car could reach 100 miles per hour, but oversteering was a problem. Eventually, German army officers were forbidden from driving the car due to the high number of fatalities they incurred. Despite that track record, a U.S. Army officer last owned this model, one of less than 100 in existence.

The 1938 Tatra T 97 is a smaller version of the T 87 (it evens shares the striking dorsal fin) and would compete with the Volkswagen. However, once Germany invaded Czechoslovakia manufacturing was halted. Only 510 had made it through production.

The likely winner of the "most odd-looking vehicle" might be the beige 1942 Mathis VL 333. Designed by Jean Andreau, the round-nosed tri-wheeled front driver can be variously described as "an egg on wheels," "the bubble car," or "the blob." This all-aluminum prototype was built under restrictive, and secretive, wartime conditions and is the only known survivor.

The cars here are not merely pretty relics of a bygone era. As Olivier points out, "All the cars are supposed to run unless we are working on them, so about 90 percent can be driven at any given time. All cars should be driven at least once a year and that is tricky to do with 70 cars. We have a mechanic who regularly starts the cars, and we also drive them home on the weekends."

With palm trees swaying in the breeze, cruising along the sun-dappled Florida coast in a classic Tatra or Delahaye sounds like a pretty good day at the Tampa Bay Automobile Museum.

Tampa Bay Automobile Museum 3301 Gateway Centre Blvd, Pinellas Park, FL 33782
www.tbauto.org

US ARMY TRANSPORTATION MUSEUM Fort Eustis, Virginia

In a saying often attributed to Napoleon, "An army travels on its stomach." The job of delivering food to the troops, along with providing them with ammunition and supplies, is a complex logistical undertaking. This task is commemorated at the United States Army Transportation Museum in Fort Eustis, Virginia, whose motto is "Nothing Happens Until Something Moves." The collection of more than three-dozen road vehicles – along with aircraft, ships, and trains – highlights the various ways the Transportation Corps fulfills its mission.

Located on the grounds of Joint Base Langley-Eustis, the 50,000 square foot main building is packed with life-sized dioramas showcasing the history of army transportation from the American Revolution through conflicts in Iraq and Afghanistan. The displays are so realistic that you expect to hear the whir of a helicopter hovering overheard.

About 2/3 of the museum's resources – the Aviation Pavilion, Truck Pavilion, Rail Pavilion and Marine Park – are outdoors.

Inside, the first vehicle to greet visitors is a 1941 Plymouth Deluxe Sedan painted in olive drab, one like this served in the Pacific during World War II. This era continues with a unique jeep known as a roadrailer. Locomotives were in short supply, so clever GIs replaced the wheels of the jeeps with the wheel rims of a 2-½ ton truck. The jeeps could now perform as locomotives hauling freight cars along the rails.

Sometimes the Army rides the waves, as exemplified by the amphibious DUKW, better known as the "Duck." Developed on the bones of a GMC 353 series 2-½ ton cargo truck, it was used to transport cargo directly from ships to shore where it could drive 45 mph on land. The Duck boat lives on as a tourist attraction in many cities across America.

No Army museum is complete without a jeep and, naturally, there are several here. The 1950s Willys M38A1 Jeep was based on the civilian model CJ-5A (Civilian Jeep-5A). It was an upgrade from the post-war M38 with a "Hurricane" F-Head engine that could climb a 69-degree incline in low gear. It's parked under the wing of a 1951 L-19 Bird Dog observation plane that was also based on a civilian vehicle, in this case a Cessna Model 170.

The Kaiser M274A2 4x4 ½-ton utility truck seems like a truck in name only. Known as the "Mechanical Mule," one of its uses was to transport weapons in Vietnam. Although it was designed to be the successor to the jeep, it looks more like a pallet on wheels.

The "Eve of Destruction" is a heavily modified 1967 Kaiser M54A1C 5-ton cargo truck that was converted into a gun truck ferrying convoys in Vietnam. It carried four .50 caliber machine guns plus an M60 machine gun as backup. With its black painted body and gothic white letters spelling out its name, it looks like an escapee from a Mad Max film set. It was shipped back to the US as a rare historical artifact.

The next revolution in Army transportation was the AM General M998 Troop Cargo Carrier or High Mobility Multi-Purpose Wheeled Vehicle (HMMWV), better known as the Humvee of Gulf War fame. This one weighs 5,380 pounds and ran on a Chevy 6.2L diesel V8.

Unfortunately, the Humvee – even in an up-armored version – did not provide enough protection for troops. The solution was the South African designed BAE Systems RG-33L Mine Resistant Ambush Protected Vehicle (MRAP).

Tractor buffs will appreciate the 1996 M-Gator 6x4. John Deere converted these from its civilian Gators as a replacement for the M274 Mechanical Mule.

Outdoors, the Rail Pavilion includes rolling stock and locomotives from World War II through the Cold War, along with some eye-popping heavy metal hauling trucks. Among them, a Fruehauf Trailer Company 45-ton tank transporter is hauling an M4A3 Sherman Tank. (The "A3" designated a Ford engine.) The big boy of the group is an M1070 8x8 tractor paired with an M1000 semitrailer capable of hauling 140,000 pounds. It's carrying a Caiman 6x6 Mine Resistant Ambush Protected Vehicle that weighs a mere 20 tons. By 2013 these MRAPs were being phased out and offered to US law enforcement agencies.

The Truck Pavilion also contains dozens of smaller vehicles including jeeps and trucks. One vehicle too large to fit into the pavilion is the post-Korean War BARC X-3 (Barge, Amphibious Resupply, Cargo). Weighing in at 193,000 pounds, it could haul 125 troops or 60 tons of supplies in one trip. The wheels alone are nine and a half feet in diameter.

The Aviation Pavilion contains one of the coolest vehicles anywhere, the bright orange GEM Model 2500 Air Car. Looking like a giant-sized bumper car from a mid-century seaside arcade, the hovercraft was developed by the Curtiss-Wright Corporation in 1959 with the hope that this technology was the wave of the future in family transport. Despite the lack of wheels, it was designed to look like a standard car, with dual headlights, taillights, and a convertible top.

The public didn't warm to the idea, but the Army thought they might have a few uses for it. They purchased two and, in that Army way of things, gave it an acronym: GEM or "Ground Effects Machine." Its twin-180hp engines that ran on aviation fuel pushed it along at 38 mph as it hovered a foot above the ground. While it showed some promise, the car didn't work well over rough terrain, making it unsuitable for extensive maneuvers. These days the hovering car of the future lives on in old *Jetsons* reruns.

Nearby, in another nod to science fiction, the Cybernetic Walking Machine robotic stick figure looks like the prototype of the All-Terrain Armored Transports that lumbered across the desert landscape in the *Star Wars* films. Built by General Electric in 1970, it would have been a success but succumbed to a flaw that classic car owners everywhere can relate to: it plowed through 50 gallons of oil per minute.

The United States Army Transportation Museum highlights a collection you will not find anywhere else, appealing to both car buffs and military enthusiasts. Between the indoor exhibits and the outdoor pavilions, a visitor can easily spend several hours here. Best of all, it's free.

Note: The museum is on the grounds of an active military base so everyone visiting will need to provide ID at the main gate for a quick background check. The driver of the vehicle must be a US citizen.

United States Army Transportation Museum 300 Washington Blvd, Besson Hall, Fort Eustis, VA 23604
www.transportation.army.mil/museum

Muscle Beach: Mopar and More

Wheels of Yesteryear Myrtle Beach, South Carolina

When Paul and Carol Cummings opened the Wheels of Yesteryear Museum in Myrtle Beach, South Carolina it was a labor of love in more ways than one: the couple has been married for more than a half century and, despite Paul's penchant for buying classic muscle cars, they still somehow get along. They showcase 40 cars in their collection, a mere sampling of the more than a hundred that are spread out over fields, barns, and chicken sheds on their property. For a time, the Panther Pink 1970 Dodge Challenger R/T was even set up on blocks in their basement so their two-year-old granddaughter could play in it. In a Technicolor display, it's now parked next to another 1970 Dodge Challenger R/T convertible in neon Green Go. Ah, the early '70s with Mopar's High Impact Paint options.

Don't let the name of the museum, which sounds like a collection of quaint Brass Era cars, fool you. The neon sign plastered to the front of the building describes the place best: "Muscle at the Beach." And those Dodge Challengers are more indicative of what you'll find here.

Despite his genteel manner, Cummings was a speedster in his day. Growing up in rural North Carolina he started drag racing while he was still a junior in high school, around the same time that he started courting Carol. When he asked Carol's mother if he could drive her daughter home from a basketball game, she took one look at his twenty-year-old Ford and his penchant for speed and said, "No, I'll drive her myself."

Although his first car was a Ford, Paul has mostly been a Mopar guy. He recalls, "I kept getting beat by Mopar cars in races at Sanford and Rockingham, so I switched over."

The collection is Mopar heaven with a heavy concentration of Hemi engines. One of Paul's favorites is a 1964 Plymouth loaded up with a Max Wedge engine that's rated at 415 horsepower. Peering under the hood at the Super Stock 426 III that runs on aviation fuel, Paul recalls somewhat wistfully, "It's the best drag car I ever ran."

Moving away from Mopar there are a few cars not often seen in museums. Although it was marketed as a luxury sedan, the 1964 Buick Riviera, with its distinctive front-end styling, qualifies as a muscle car per Paul. It's hard to ignore the 360 horsepower V-8 parked under the hood.

One car that gets a few chuckles is the 1973 AMC Gremlin X. Its V-8 puts out a bit less than the Riviera, but it also packs a lot less weight. A placard on the vehicle refers to it as "the poor man's Corvette."

The red 1961 Chevy Biscayne, with a rare 409 engine, is a powerful model that was factory built for drag racing, which is why it lacks a back seat. The hood on this one, like many others, is propped open;

fans who visit Wheels of Yesteryear are just as interested in what powers each car as what they look like on the outside.

A reading room in the museum is packed with a donated set of binders full of vintage car ads taken from old magazines. You could easily spend a day leafing through them. The walls are outfitted with so many memorabilia – hubcaps, steering wheels, license plates, and the like – that it's almost hard to notice the rough-hewn wood that was sourced from Paul's father's farm. Perhaps starting him on his way to being a world-class collector his father once told him, "If you don't need your junk, don't throw it away. Someone else might want it."

What's striking about the museum is that many cars are noted as survivors and are in their original condition. Paul says, "The most positive comments we get are from people who appreciate that. For many folks it's a real memory lane here." Even when he does a repaint, he applies original colors. On the cars he used for racing many of the interiors are pristine because he had them removed for racing and placed back later.

With the continually increasing interest in muscle cars the collection is very valuable right now. But that wasn't always the case. Paul says, "I bought most of the cars in the '70s when they were a few years old. You could pick up a lot of them for only $800." Oh, if that were the case now.

Because they have so many cars still back in the barn, they shut down for two weeks at the end of January and rotate about a dozen cars each year so there is something new for the many repeat visitors who stop in on the way to their beach vacations.

When Paul is asked if he was still buying cars Carol's eyes light up and she blurts out, "I hope not!" Paul chuckles somewhat sheepishly, "Well, you asked me at the wrong time. Let's step over here to talk about it." It appears that Paul is not finished in his quest for muscle cars at the beach.

Wheels of Yesteryear 413 Hospitality Lane, Myrtle Beach, SC 29579 www.WheelsOfYesteryearMB.com

CENTRAL UNITED STATES

MOTORING TO AUBURN, INDIANA

AUBURN CORD DUESENBERG AUTOMOBILE MUSEUM
EARLY FORD V8 FOUNDATION MUSEUM
NATIONAL AUTO & TRUCK MUSEUM
Auburn, IN

Due to its rich automotive heritage, the town of Auburn, located in northeast Indiana, is known as the "Home of the Classics" and attracts visitors from around the world to see its sterling array of classic car museums. At the dawn of the automotive era, it was an early rival to Detroit. A trio of museums and special events will keep a classic car buff busy here.

Auburn Cord Duesenberg Automobile Museum

During the 1920s and '30s local auto magnate EL Cord owned the Auburn and Duesenberg marques, so start your classic journey at the Auburn Cord Duesenberg Automobile Museum, an impressive collection of 130 vehicles spread out over a three-story office building that was occupied by the Auburn Automobile Company.

Even in the rarefied air of upscale classic car museums, it's a real head turner. The initial impact is at the ground level, where the beautifully restored former circa 1929 Art Deco showroom, with its geometric terrazzo floor and grand center staircase, provides a splendid backdrop for displaying some of the most beautiful vehicles to ever hit the open road.

It wasn't always a smooth ride though; after the company shut down during the Great Depression, the 22 Italian chandeliers that now grace the ceiling were once destined for the trash heap before an enterprising employee decided to save them. Things turned around in the 1970s when a group of automotive enthusiasts purchased the then vacant building and opened the Auburn Cord Duesenberg Automobile Museum on July 6, 1974. (Ironically, when the museum celebrated its 45th year of existence in 2019, it boasted a longer track record than the car companies that it commemorates.)

The ground floor was the original corporate showroom where new Auburn models were revealed to dealers in the 1930s. Cars on this level include a tropical colored yellow-and-red 1931 Cord drophead coupe, 1932 Duesenberg Model J, and a 1936 Auburn 852 Phaeton.

The Duesenberg brothers, Fred and August, were innovative car makers in the 1920s. However, the company was not a financial success until E.L. Cord purchased a controlling interest in 1926 and encouraged them to make the finest car in the world. The Duesenbergs of the "Cord" era, particularly the high-end Model J, are some of the most deluxe automobiles ever built in America and, with owners like silver screen stars Clark Gable and Gary Cooper, were the must-have celebrity car of the era.

A dozen are on display in all their chromed glory. One of the silkiest is a stunning two-tone turquoise and jade 1930 Duesenberg Model J convertible sedan that features a fold-down bar with a crystal decanter in the backseat; the hood alone looks long enough to serve comfortably as a picnic table for a large family gathering. A 1931 model nearby came equipped with a Tiffany make-up set.

However, even luxury car buyers were affected by the Great Depression as Auburn, Cord, and Duesenberg motored on through the 1930s, fighting a rearguard action to stay in business. Innovative hidden headlights (a feature that wouldn't be seen again for decades) imparted a sleek appearance to the "coffin" nose on the 1936 Cord 810. This car was the height of pre-war automotive styling. However, perhaps the coffin reference was a precursor of what was to come as the company closed its doors the following year.

A separate area is devoted to cars designed by Gordon Buehrig, who became Duesenberg's chief designer at the tender age of 25. Among his creations are a 1931 Duesenberg Model J Beverly saloon, with its distinctive low silhouette and raked windscreen. Other cars of his design are a 1935 Auburn 851 Speedster and a one-of-a-kind 1948 Tasco from The American Sports Car Company.

However, it's not all Auburns, Cords, and Duesenbergs at their namesake museum. The "Gallery of Special Interest Automobiles" features unusual classics like a rare 1952 Cisitalia 202 Gran Sport and a 1933 Checker Cab from the year that Cord acquired the Checker Cab company.

A section devoted to cars manufactured in Indiana includes an 1894 Black, 1920 Lexington Minute Man Six, and a 1922 Haynes. The focus narrows to Auburn-produced automobiles with a 1907 Kiblinger, 1910 Zimmerman, and a 1913 Imp. Iconic American architect Frank Lloyd Wright was a car buff, and two of his former vehicles are on display: painted in Wright's signature "Cherokee Red" are his 1930 Cord L-29 Cabriolet and a diminutive 1952 Crosley.

In promotional materials for the Cord Corporation Wright observed, "The proportion and lines of the Cord come nearer expressing the beauty of both science and logic than any car I have ever seen."

The Hall of Technology provides up-close views of several engines, along with hands-on displays where budding mechanics can spin handles and push buttons to learn about things like axle ratios and prop shafts. The Design Studios area takes visitors inside the styling process for new automobiles with clay models and original sketches of proposed designs for everything from hubcaps to steering wheels.

National Auto & Truck Museum

The National Auto & Truck Museum is adjacent to the ACD Museum in the circa 1920s factory buildings of the Auburn Automobile Company, including the space where the front-wheel-drive Cord L-29 was developed. More than 100 automobiles and trucks are on display – along with hundreds of model cars – and, in a nod to Cord's former ownership of Checker Cabs, a row of vintage taxis, along with some quirky vehicles.

One such oddity is a bright red and chrome 1940 GM Futurliner #10. Looking like a cross between a Flash Gordon-era Airstream and a bus, 12 of these crisscrossed the USA in GM's Parade of Progress science and technology exhibition during the 1940s and '50s. Nearby is a 1981 DeLorean, in rare factory red paint over its stainless-steel exterior. A 1965 Mustang Fastback 2+2 is kitted with a 185hp Wankel rotary engine, a concept that didn't catch on for the pony car. An airflow design series 1938 Dodge Model RX-70 in Texaco livery is a highlight in the truck section.

Also located in the facility is the National Automotive & Truck Model & Toy Museum that highlights toy, pedal, and model cars and trucks ranging from 1894 to the present.

Early Ford V8 Foundation Museum

For Ford fans, a worthwhile side trip in Auburn is the Early Ford V8 Foundation Museum that preserves Ford Motor Company history from 1932 through 1953. It underwent a major expansion that tripled its size in late 2018, with the unveiling of a new addition to the museum, a replica of the Ford Rotunda that appeared at the 1934 Chicago World's Fair, giving it more space to showcase Ford.

Inside, there are more than 50 vehicles including a re-created vintage dealership named Floyd Motors that showcases 18 1936 Fords, an example of every model built that year. The most unusual of which is a 1936 Tudor Sedan made of stainless steel for promotional purposes that sits on a rotating turntable in the Rotunda. Another highlight is a 1940 Lincoln Continental Cabriolet.

The most exciting time to visit Auburn is during the annual Auburn Cord Duesenberg Festival that straddles the last week of August and first week of September. Billed as "The World's Greatest Classic Car Show & Festival," you'll just have to decide for yourself.

Auburn Cord Duesenberg Automobile Museum 1600 South Wayne Street, Auburn, IN 46706
    www.AutomobileMuseum.org

National Auto & Truck Museum 1000 Gordon M. Buehrig Place, Auburn, IN 46706
    natmus.org

Early Ford V8 Foundation Museum 2181 Rotunda Drive, Auburn, IN 46706
    www.fordv8foundation.org

Lapping Up the "Greatest Spectacle in Racing"

Indianapolis Motor Speedway Museum Indianapolis, Indiana

To race fans, nothing kicks off summer like the annual Memorial Day Weekend running of the Indianapolis 500 car race. Begun in 1911, the "Indy 500" is one of the premier auto races in the world with a roster of champions that includes legends Mario Andretti, brothers Bobby and Al Unser, A. J. Foyt, and the Brazilian Hélio Castroneves.

The track is traditionally referred to as "The Brickyard," hearkening back to 1911 when 3.2 million paving bricks were laid over the existing crushed stone and tar surface. The track has been covered over with asphalt since then, however a 36-inch strip of the original brick at the start/finish line remains as an homage to the pioneering age of racing.

Although the race occurs during a single day, fans can still experience a vicarious thrill year-round by visiting the Indianapolis Motor Speedway Museum. Located within the infield of the iconic track, more than 70 cars on display, with their scrapes and dents, tell the history of the rugged event.

More than two dozen of the cars in the museum are Indy 500 winners while memorabilia including racing helmets, programs, track-worn tires, and trophies fill cases along the walls. The coveted Borg-Warner trophy sits nestled among the winning cars: the sterling silver five-foot-tall iconic bas-relief sculpture features a 3D-sculpted face of every winning driver of the Indy 500. The original trophy stays here, while the champion driver receives a replica.

The museum boasts two cars that appear on the prestigious 24-car National Historic Vehicle Register that is selected by the Historic Vehicle Association: the 1911 Marmon Wasp that won the inaugural Indianapolis 500 in 1911 and the maroon 1938 Maserati 8CTF known as the "Boyle Special." The latter captured the Indy 500 checkered flag in both 1939 and 1940 and is considered the most successful car in the history of the race.

A. J. Foyt is the only driver to have won the race four times and he is well-represented here with the Foyt "Coyote," in which he won his historic fourth Indy 500 in 1977. Parked next to it is New Jersey native Mark Donohue's McLaren M-16B, first across the finish line in 1972. Donohue's car was the shape of things to come: the aerodynamic bolt-on wings pushed it to a then-record speed of 162.9 miles per hour.

The Honda-powered car driven by rookie Alexander Rossi won the 100th running of the race in 2016. (Although the event started in 1911, races were suspended during wartime.) Upon crossing the finish line Rossi ran out of fuel and had to be towed back to Victory Lane for the traditional glass of milk drunk by the winning driver.

The Dallara/Honda driven by British racer Dan Wheldon to victory in 2011 – his second win here – is a poignant reminder of the dangers of high-speed auto racing. Weldon was killed in an accident later that same year at the Las Vegas Motor Speedway at the age of 33 – a promising career and life cut way too short.

What makes these historic cars even more remarkable is that most of them still run; each year a few are brought out for a few spins around the track during pre-race festivities.

A "please touch" area includes the Offenhauser Parts Petting Zoo, where kids can touch and feel parts like a camshaft or crankcase from the legendary Offenhauser engine. Cars with "Offy" technology dominated open-wheel racing from the 1930s through the 1970s.

While the museum overlooks the racing track and grandstands, for an up-close view take a mini-bus tour of the 2 ½-mile oval track. Visitors stop at the start/finish line where they can emulate their favorite winning drivers and "kiss the bricks," a strip of circa 1909 bricks that remain from the original racing surface. But you'll have to bring your own glass of milk.

Indianapolis Motor Speedway Museum 4790 W. 16th Street, Speedway IN 46224
www.IndyRacingMuseum.org

LIFE IN THE FAST LANE:
A WORLD TOUR OF CARS IN NASHVILLE

LANE MOTOR MUSEUM Nashville, Tennessee

If I ever write a story about the ten most unusual vehicles I've come across in motor museums, half of these oddities might be located at the Lane Motor Museum in Nashville, Tennessee. In a town that's famous for its country music singers and guitar slingers, the Lane is a world-class attraction in its own right. With its "Unique Cars from A to Z" mantra, there are vehicles for almost every letter of the alphabet.

To give an idea of the breadth of the collection, the letter "S" alone includes the following marques: Saab, Sabra, Schmitty, SEAB, Simca, Skoda, smart, Steyr, Subaru, and Suzuki.

The museum claims to offer the largest collection of European cars on American soil but there is so much more – the United States and Asia are also well represented. National flags hanging from the rafters of the former Sunbeam commercial bread bakery designate areas for cars from the UK, Sweden, Japan, Czechoslovakia, and more.

The main floor displays approximately 150 cars and motorcycles, from a collection of more than 500 vehicles. They are spaced apart so visitors can walk around them and peer inside – no velvet ropes separate the cars from their fans.

This is a working museum; car aficionado Jeff Lane, who founded the museum in 2002, tries to keep every car in running condition to preserve their unique automotive heritage for future generations to enjoy. He started working on cars at the tender age of 12, when he helped his father restore a 1955 MG TF 1500. The vehicle, in which he also passed his driving license test, is one of the first cars visitors see upon entering the museum.

British Beauties

Some of Lane's other favorite British cars in the collection include: a 1970 Lotus Elan (which looks familiar to any fan of Emma Peel on *The Avengers*), a 1981 Caterham Super Seven roadster and a 1965 Peel (no relation to Emma) Trident microcar built on the Isle of Man. While the tight confines of the bubble-top Trident can technically fit two people, they better really get along.

Other unusual British cars here include a 1922 ABC roadster and a duo of three-wheeled vehicles including a 1933 BSA (Birmingham Small Arms) TW33-9 Special Sports and a 1959 Scootacar MK-I. The latter was powered by a Villiers 9E motor to achieve 8.5 hp.

A vehicle that would be unusual to find nestled in a museum on either side of the Atlantic is the more prosaic 1968 Commer (division of Rootes) Imp delivery van that was assembled in Scotland.

Eclectic (And Electric) Engineering

Lane has had a long fascination with the Czech-built Tatra. He states, "I was drawn to Tatras because of their very advanced engineering. We have 20 Tatras in the collection, the largest group of Tatras in the United States." The 1947 Tatra T-87 Saloon makes visitors do a double-take with its Tuckeresque features, including a sleek aerodynamic body, three headlights and an air-cooled, rear-mounted engine that predated the more famous Tucker.

A banner hanging from the rafters declares "Electric Cars, Always the Car of the Future." While in 2021 that future appears to be finally arriving, several electric pioneers from the past are on view including a 1959 Henney Kilowatt. This oddity, based on specially ordered Renault Dauphines that were delivered without power trains, was produced by a US-based consortium that included the Henney Motor Company. Although the car never sparked much interest, its technology was a precursor to electric vehicles like GM's EV1.

Aerocars/Nautocars

If your motoring interests lean more to aeronautics, the one-off Jupiter rocket car fits the bill. Born out of the 1960s Southern California hot rod "Kustom Kulture," the vehicle was built in 1961 by the legendary custom fabricator Kenny Howard, who went by the nom de plume Von Dutch. Reportedly built as a prop for a film that never made it into production, it was cleverly constructed out of an aluminum 120-gallon belly tank from a United States Air Force F-86 Sabre jet fighter. Despite its fancy Space Age moniker, the open-air two-seater is powered by a more down to earth 74 cid Harley-Davidson UL Flat Head air-cooled engine.

A prior exhibit was called "Wingless Wonders-Propellor Drive Vehicles That Never Took Off." One of the highlights is the rather steampunk looking French 1932 Helicron. A large propeller is attached to the front of the one-of-a-kind rear-steering wooden vehicle that was uncovered in a barn in 2000. After its restoration, the car passed French safety inspections with a non-original air-cooled Citroën GS engine and is now road-worthy, although, despite the propeller, it won't get airborne.

Traveling from land to sea, there are nine amphibious vehicles in the collection with the 1964 Amphicar being one of the more mainstream swimmers of this eclectic lot that includes a 1987 LuAZ 967M Jeep-like Soviet Army vehicle – the driver could steer the car from a prone position in case they were being shot at – and an amphibious 1978 Citroën 2CV.

The strangest fish here is the 1961 Chevrolet Corphibian. Engineers Richard Hulten and Roger Holm fabricated the floating prototype out of a Corvair Loadside pickup. The regular Corvair air-cooled rear-mounted engine drove the twin propellers. Although they tagged the car as a Chevy, the company wasn't interested in it; this is the last remnant of a truly unique idea.

Dotty Drivers

Other unusual vehicles include a 1951 Hoffmann, a three-wheeled German contraption derived from hardware store and junkyard parts. With its wide front and rear-wheel steering, it defied any expectations of safety and was, fortunately, not manufactured in bulk. Its restorer likened driving it to "a drunk leaving a hotel bar."

The open-top 1958 SMZ S3A Invalidka car was available through the government social care system to Russian veterans who had been injured in World War II.

Vintage diagnostic testing equipment lines the walls to round out the collection. The museum is also very kid-friendly with a large play area chockful of toy cars, which can come in handy because you may be here for a while.

Special Exhibits And "Vault Tours"

An additional 200 vehicles are located downstairs where guided Vault Tours (with limited capacity) are offered most weekends. It's best to check ahead for the schedule if that's what you're coming for.

Throughout the year vehicles are rotated in for special exhibits like "Stretch to Fit: Fabric Covered Cars" and "A Recipe For Speed: Open Wheel Racing."

Note: The museum constantly rotates through the vehicles on display so, if there is something you absolutely must see, call ahead.

Lane Motor Museum 702 Murfreesboro Pike, Nashville, TN 37210

www.LaneMotorMuseum.org

DREAMING BIG IN KANSAS
AT THE MIDWEST DREAM CAR COLLECTION

MIDWEST DREAM CAR COLLECTION Manhattan, Kansas

When Dorothy Gale uttered the words, "Toto, I have a feeling we're not in Kansas anymore," she could have been speaking about the Midwest Dream Car Collection instead of the land of Oz. However, this magical spot *is* in Kansas – the college town of Manhattan, to be exact. The museum opened in 2019 as a place to store the burgeoning collection of tech entrepreneurs Ward and Brenda Morgan. In 2017 they began collecting cars and, within 18 months, they were searching for a spot to park 60 vehicles. Yeesh, it takes me 18 months just to pick new wiper blades.

The Morgans purchased a 54,000 square foot former supermarket to provide a cavernous spot for their burgeoning collection. We toured the museum with Executive Director Chris Gergeni and

Director of Vehicle Operations Doug Meloan, who came in on a day that the museum was closed to fit into our tight cross-country road trip schedule.

Two things are evident upon entering. First, they resisted the urge to cram in as many cars as possible, allowing visitors to walk all the way around them. Second, there are no ropes to keep visitors at a distance, so they can poke their head inside the vehicles. According to Gergeni, "From day one we wanted this to be an open museum with no barriers." Unlike most museums (of any type) they also provide a self-serve bar with wine and beer on tap available for purchase.

Chronologically the vehicles range from a 1907 Ford Model R to a 2018 Dodge Challenger SRT Demon with a supercharged 6.2-liter Hemi V8 capable of 840 hp. A trio of vehicles reveal the wide breadth of this collection: a Springfield, Massachusetts built 1925 Rolls-Royce Silver Ghost; 1950 Ford F1 Pickup Truck; and a 1973 Volkswagen Type 181, aka "The Thing."

Pre-war elegance is epitomized by a 1931 Packard Series 840 convertible coupe; 1932 Packard 902 coupe roadster; and a 1937 Cord 812 supercharged cabriolet. The post-war years aren't too shabby either with a 1948 Chrysler New Yorker Town and Country Woodie convertible; 1956 Continental Mark II; and a 1958 Cadillac Eldorado Biarritz convertible.

When attending auctions, Ward Morgan takes note of which cars people cluster around and often bids on those vehicles. The result is a museum filled with crowd pleasers.

Two of those head turning cars are the his-and-her 1966 Ford Mustang convertibles created for Sonny & Cher by the "King of Kustomizers," George Barris. They were pulled from the production line at the San Jose plant, hence the consecutive serial numbers.

As expected, Cher's is more flamboyant. The Hot Candy Pink pony car boasts an interior of white ermine fur trimmed with pink suede. In comparison, Sonny's Mustang, painted in Murano Gold with suede side panels, looks a bit more prosaic. In both cars you can sink your mod-inspired Beatles boots into the plush shag carpeting.

According to Gergeni, "While boomers crowd around the Mustangs, the younger generation is more likely to ask, 'Who are Sonny and Cher?'"

Despite the popularity of the station wagon in the post-war "let's move out to the suburbs decades" they aren't often found in museums. On display here is a gorgeous Seaspray Green and Cameo Ivory 1959 Pontiac Catalina Safari station wagon, made at the height of the station wagon era. The 389 cubic-inch Tempest V8 with the optional factory correct "Tri-Power" triple two-barrel carburetor cranked out 330 horsepower.

If you remember riding backwards on road trips, the flip-up rear facing third row seat will induce a bout of nostalgia, or, in the case of some young riders, nausea. Dad didn't care because he was in the driver's seat, about a mile away, threatening to "turn this car around" if your siblings in the second row didn't stop already with the spitballs.

A rare car to see in a museum – or anywhere – is the 1979 Chrysler 300. Chrysler was on the verge of bankruptcy when they introduced the 300 series, which was a jazzed-up Cordoba coupe. All were painted in Spinnaker White (Chianti Red was an option in Canada) with interiors swaddled in plush, dare I say, Corinthian leather. Despite smart styling and a hefty 360 ci, 195 hp V8, timing was less than ideal. This 300 debuted amidst the late 70s gas crisis, when your fill ups were restricted to odd/even days, corresponding to the last digit of your license plate.

I lusted after Bricklins during my misspent teen years, so it was a joy to see a 1975 Bricklin SV-1 in Safety Orange. The SV designation stood for "Safety Vehicle." Had I known that in high school I might not have been as enamored of the sleek car. Powered by a Ford Windsor V-8 that reached 175 horsepower, the gull wing doors were a precursor to the car parked beside it – a 1981 DeLorean DMC-12. Although the latter's PRV (Peugeot, Renault, Volvo) V-6 produced a not-so-sleek 130 horsepower. Meloan recalls, "Every mistake Bricklin made, DeLorean made ten years later."

I may be a sentimental fool but after seeing the Bricklin here, 40 years later, I still want to drive one.

The 1952 Manta Ray concept car was built by aircraft designers Glenn Hire and Vernon Antoine in a garage in Whittier, California. It was inspired by Harley Earl's iconic 1951 Buick LeSabre concept car as evidenced by the round central grille and flamboyant aircraft styling. There are triple taillights, one below each fin.

Despite publicity in *Motor Trend* and *Popular Science*, the car never made it into production beyond this prototype. One of a handful of loaner cars on display, it's owned by the Lacer family of Junction City, Kansas whose patriarch, L.L. "Peanuts" Lacer, found it at a Topeka used car dealership in the late 1950s. How it got there is a mystery.

The museum is also focused on educating the public about cars. The Morgan Family Lecture Series brings in expert guest speakers on a variety of topics including automotive art, culture, and history. They are also seeking to attract the next generation to the hobby in the Kids Studio where 5- to 11-year-olds work on auto related crafts and projects.

Cars and coffee are on Saturday mornings while, during Open Hood Sunday on the last Sunday of the month, museum Master Technician Nick Poell pops up the hood on selected vehicles to talk about them. During regular hours visitors can watch through a plate glass window as Poell works on cars in the mechanic's shop.

The Midwest Dream Car Collection is aptly named. We might have been in Kansas, but I definitely felt like I had landed in Oz, if they had cars, that is.

Midwest Dream Car Collection 3007 Anderson Ave., Manhattan, KS 66503

MidwestDreamCarCollection.org

FLOODED ENGINES IN WISCONSIN

MIDWEST MICROCAR MUSEUM Mazomanie, Wisconsin

You think you have problems with your single vehicle restoration? Imagine trying to restore an entire museum's worth of vehicles. In August 2018, massive summer rainstorms blew through central Wisconsin dropping 17 inches of rain in a little over 2 hours. The effect was severe in the village of Mazomanie as Black Earth Creek overflowed its banks with a 500-year flood, deluging the 19th-century brick structure housing the Midwest Microcar Museum. The surge inundated the museum with more than 3 feet of water, partially submerging more than a dozen microcars and motorcycles.

The museum had been founded only three years earlier by German immigrants Carlo and Ingrid Krause. (Carlo arrived in the United States with his family as a three-year-old and Ingrid later as an adult.) In the late 1950s Carlo returned to Germany to get his university degree in Berlin, fell in love with the microcars then gracing the roads and began collecting them. Carlo passed away in 2019, but Ingrid continues the successful businessman's life mantra "Nothing Ventured, Nothing Gained" as she moves forward with this unique museum.

That mantra was put to the test after the flood. The receding waters left behind a slurry of oil and fluids coating the floor and cars that had to be cleaned up while the damage to the vehicles was assessed. In an ironic twist, the Amphicar was the only vehicle still full of water. The windows of the sealed amphibious vehicle had been left open in the museum, so it retained all the flood water that poured into it.

As Ingrid recalls, "We felt like giving up. We had just fixed up a 1958 Nobel 200 that we purchased at the Bruce Weiner microcar auction. It had only been on the floor for two weeks before it got flooded."

After deciding to move forward and fix the cars and the museum, the Krauses contacted local auto restorer Chris Beebe to do the work that was very challenging, to say the least.

According to Beebe, "There were no manuals to fix anything, so I learned as I went along." Fortunately, the damage to the cars wasn't as bad as it first looked. Although they required a massive clean-up Beebe says, "We didn't have to replace any parts except upholstery."

But enough about the flood. After a three-year hiatus the museum recently reopened with a splash so let's look at the vehicles. The two-dozen microcars are arrayed over two floors in a former blacksmith shop. When the Krauses bought the building, it already had an exterior scissor lift so they could move the cars up to the second floor. Judging by the diminutive size of the lift, it's fortunate they weren't moving Packards or Cadillacs.

A few of the cars here, like the 1955 Messerschmitt KR200 and 1958 BMW Isetta, are ones you'll come across as the oddball microcar in larger museums but, this being a specialty museum, those cars are of the more normal variety here. The Krauses have done an exemplary job of seeking out the unusual and obscure to round out their collection with cars that you are not likely to see anywhere else.

One such example is the 1953 Rovin that was built by brothers Raoul and Robert Marquis in Rovin, France. They had been car manufacturers before World War II, but during post-war austerity realized the need for an inexpensive mode of transportation. They built 1,200 vehicles, with some modifications, between 1946 and 1959. The first year's model didn't even include doors and offered only a single headlight for illumination. The final model on display here sported a 13 hp engine that propelled it to 53 mph.

Moving forward in time, the Nevco Electric Gizmo was launched at the dawn of the new millennium. Looking like something that would be driven around a small village by a meter reader, the single-passenger vehicle was designed for running errands on local roads where it could allegedly reach 40 miles per hour. Over half the weight was attributed to the battery. At a cost of $8-12,000 it didn't catch on with the public.

Whenever a new James Bond movie is released there's much hoopla in the car world about Bond cars, but no one will confuse the 1953 Bond Minicar "shopping car" with one the intrepid 007 would be caught dead in. One of Ingrid Krause's favorite cars, it was originally developed in England by Bond, Lawrence Bond, as a motorcycle/car hybrid.

The hood is raised and a glance at the simple mechanics reminds me of the halcyon days of my youth when cars were so much easier to work on; back then when you looked inside the engine bay you could see your feet poking out underneath.

Even more basic is the Valmobile Fold-A-Way Motor Scooter. Picture an actual working motorized vehicle that folds up into its own roughly two-foot by one-foot case that you could take on a plane as carry-on luggage. Developed by Frenchman Victor Bouggart, the name roughly translates as mobile suitcase.

Among the other cars on display are a 1941 Crosley Sedan CB41, 1957 Heinkel Kabine 153, 1956 Mochet, and a 1964 Goggomobil T250.

Just 100 feet west of the car collection, the museum renovated another brick industrial building to house their Vintage Cycle Room. Despite the name there are a few autos here too. A Cold War relic among the two-wheelers is a 1980 MZ TS 150 East German border patrol motorcycle. Ingrid, who was raised in West Germany, says, "In the west we didn't need such patrols. We said come on over."

Looking at the restored cars in the newly reopened museum Chris Beebe beams like a proud papa. He recalls, "Some cars like the Reliant Regal were as frustrating as all get out – I couldn't believe the engineering that went into it – but frustration is part of the game." That's a statement that any car restorer, flood, or no flood, can attest to.

While there aren't regular operating hours, the museum is typically open three or four weekends a month.

Midwest Microcar Museum 103 Crescent St, Mazomanie, WI 53560

www.MidwestMicrocarMuseum.com

Get Your Kicks
at the National Corvette Museum

National Corvette Museum Bowling Green, Kentucky

There's no more iconic road in America than Route 66, so it makes sense that when the *Route 66* television show first hit the small screen in 1960, our two intrepid heroes drove that most iconic of American sports cars – a brand new Corvette – as they roamed across the country in search of adventure. The view of the car as it crossed the sun-kissed desert in Arizona, or glided along the neon lit Hollywood Boulevard, was embedded in the minds of television viewers – and potential buyers – every week.

Its continued production almost 70 years after its 1953 debut is a testament to its sporting bona fides and desirability. With a nod to the musician Prince, a meme floats around the internet: it's a photo of a striking red Corvette sports car with the caption, "They Don't

Write Songs About Volvos." For a vehicle old enough to collect Social Security, that's quite an achievement.

The legacy of America's sports car lives on at the National Corvette Museum in Bowling Green, Kentucky. It's located a half-mile south of the Bowling Green Assembly Plant, where General Motors has built all Corvettes sold worldwide since 1981. The museum opened in 1994 and showcases more than 80 Corvettes, starting with the car's birth in 1953, up through the latest model Corvette in the entrance foyer, in which visitors can sit for a photo op. The structure is immediately recognizable by its Skydome, a canary-yellow 100-foot-high conical structure, pierced by a red spire that is its signature motif. Inside, the museum is divided into sections – Nostalgia, Mobil Gas Station, Route 66, Dealership, Performance/ Racing, Design/Engineering, Maintenance/Preservation and others – that highlight various aspects of the car's history.

If you've already heard of the museum, it's likely due to an event that occurred on February 12, 2014. That night, a giant 60-foot by 40-foot sinkhole opened underneath the Skydome's floor, swallowing eight vintage Corvettes 30 feet beneath the earth's surface. The sinkhole was the lead item on news outlets around the world, putting the National Corvette Museum on the map.

Due to the publicity, attendance soared within days of the sinkhole. (Remarkably, the museum was closed for only one day to cordon off the area and provide a viewing window.) Rather than shirking from that night's events, on the second anniversary of the collapse the museum opened a new exhibit titled "Corvette Cave In! The Skydome Sinkhole Experience" that, with all its geological material, resembles something from a natural history museum.

Inside the renovated Skydome, three of the mangled cars that were beyond restoration are coated with powdery evidence of the area's terra cotta-colored soil still encrusted on them. Fortunately, another three of the damaged Corvettes were salvageable. Two of them – a 1992 model that was the 1,000,000th Corvette built and a 2009 ZR1 Blue Devil – have been restored and are displayed next to their damaged brethren. The third – a 1962 Corvette in Tuxedo

Black – was restored at the museum under the inquisitive eyes of visitors. It was unveiled on the fourth anniversary of the collapse.

Despite its legendary status today, the Corvette had a relatively modest start. In 1953, the original run was just 300 Corvettes that were hand-built in Flint, Michigan, the only year the cars were produced there. They were all painted Polo White, and featured a red interior, black canvas top and automatic transmission – number 262 of that limited inaugural year run is on display. Parked next to it is a model from 1954, when production increased twelve-fold to 3,640 cars that were built in St. Louis, Missouri.

The Corvette wasn't always the roaring success we know today. Early 'Vettes were underpowered and achieved disappointing sales; GM almost pulled the plug in the late 1950s. The plant was designed with an annual capacity of 10,000 units in mind, but GM didn't reach that goal until 1960, a year when all the cars produced were convertibles.

Ironically, it took a Russian émigré to rev up America's Sports Car and keep it humming. Zora Arkus-Duntov joined General Motors in 1953, and ultimately came to work on the Corvette. The man, who would eventually become known as the "Godfather of the Corvette," emphasized performance, which was just the tune-up the brand needed. Visitors to the museum can see the only Corvette ever owned by Arkus-Duntov: a 1974 model. True to his engineering roots, he modified the production model into an even higher performance vehicle.

There are several unique models on display. One is a sleek 1968 Astro-Vette that would look at home in a *Flash Gordon* movie. It was built to see how aerodynamically slippery the sports car could be designed. As bizarre as it may have looked in 1968, by 1973 Corvettes dropped their chrome front bumpers and took on the prototype's polyurethane front end – the following year the rear bumper followed suit.

The exhibit "Astro-Enthusiast: Corvettes and Rockets" draws an interesting parallel with events of the time. Corvettes and the burgeoning Space Age were made for each other; the sleek automobiles were the terrestrial equivalent of the rockets launching satellites, chimpanzees, and eventually man into outer space. Chevrolet recognized the benefits early on of association with the tales of derring-do emanating from America's space program.

After Alan Shepard became the first American in space, General Motors presented the astronaut a brand new white 1962 Corvette. The roster of the Cape Kennedy Corvette Club eventually included many astronauts. A copy of Neil Armstrong's signed membership application, noting his ownership of a silver 1968 Corvette convertible, is on display along with other memorabilia. Visitors can view mission patches and a National Corvette Museum flag that was flown into space by a later generation of astronauts.

Under a team led by legendary racer Tommy Morrison, the 1989 Corvette ZR-1 set a 24-Hour Speed Endurance world record by averaging 175.885 mph (283.061 kph) on a wet racetrack in Fort Stockton, Texas. The race-prepared stock LT5 V8 5.7-liter displacement 32-valve aluminum engine was designed by the Lotus Group of the UK and built in the US for the attempt. The car also features a ZF six-speed manual gearbox and Goodyear 12.0 x 17 special radial tires that held up during the effort, even helping to avoid one curious coyote who had strayed onto the fenceless track.

Beyond ogling sleek cars, there are many interactive exhibits including Corvette trivia touch screens and a driving simulator. Video screens throughout the museum show the car in action, along with narrative from Corvette designers and engineers. There's also a KidZone with Pat's Super Service Center. Here children can change the car's tires, air filter and exhaust. In addition, a Just in Time Assembly Line encourages people to work together to put wheels on vehicles moving down the line.

National Corvette Museum 350 Corvette Drive, Bowling Green, KY 42101
www.CorvetteMuseum.org

From Buggy Whips to American Muscle Cars

Pontiac-Oakland Museum Pontiac, Illinois

There aren't too many places where Fiero body panels are proudly displayed on the walls, but the Pontiac-Oakland Museum & Resource Center in Pontiac, Illinois is one of them. This incredible collection illustrates how one man's obsession can grow into a significant museum. In this case, Tim Dye has been accumulating all things Pontiac related since his teen years and is supported in his quest by his always patient wife Penny.

The Pontiac, Illinois location for the museum leads many visitors to assume the car was made here, but they were not. The Dyes lived in Broken Arrow, Oklahoma and needed more space for their rapidly growing collection. While driving south after attending a car show near Chicago, they passed through town and made a few inquiries. When Robert Russell, the mayor of Pontiac, learned of their plans he attracted them to his charming downtown with an offer of a building to house the museum. The result is an immaculately curated collection that provides a thrill to any auto aficionado cruising along nearby Route 66.

The Oakland Motor Car Company started out in 1907 in Pontiac, Michigan and was a subsidiary of the Pontiac Buggy Company. Dating back to those early roots, an 1890s Pontiac Buggy (one of only two that exist) is on view. After being gobbled up by General Motors, Oakland started producing Pontiac automobiles, a respected name that lived on until its sad demise in 2010. The brand that arguably launched the muscle car era with the 1964 GTO was no more, making it even more important to preserve the Pontiac legacy. A 1965 GTO in the museum recalls those heady days.

A 1964 Pontiac Parisienne Safari Station Wagon is set up in such a lifelike camping tableau with a one of those ubiquitous Scotch coolers, Coleman stove and faux fire, that you can almost smell the wieners roasting. The wagon was built in Canada, so it features a Chevrolet drive train and chassis. A frequent feature at the museum is a black-and-gold 1976 Pontiac Trans Am 50th Anniversary Edition. It will get the motor running of anyone who lusted after one of these bad boys when they were teenagers. The second-generation Firebird went on to cinematic fame in *Smokey and the Bandit* and *Rocky II*, creating a new generation of Trans Am fans.

Any type of Pontiac memorabilia you can think of is here including uniforms from sports teams Pontiac sponsored, vintage advertising, dinnerware, Indian headdresses used for marketing, toy cars by year and so much more. The collection of Pontiac logos, trim and hubcaps alone could fill a small barn.

The largest Pontiac-Oakland reference library in the world contains thousands of documents including owner's manuals, marketing materials, service manuals, books, and magazines. It was fun to leaf through the materials and find the original owner's manual and sales brochure for my first car, a Pontiac Firebird. Tim has spread his collecting net so wide he even has loads of material related to the Native American Chief Pontiac. Because Tim's actual collection is larger than the museum, some of the cars are rotated out frequently, creating a new visitor experience every time. A few of the models that are always on display include the 1890s Pontiac buggy, 1931 Oakland Sport Coupe (it was the last model year for Oakland) and the camping display with the 1964 station wagon.

Tim's obsession with Pontiac reminds me of a song called Tulsa Time that's been recorded over the years by Don Williams and Eric Clapton about someone leaving Oklahoma driving a Pontiac. Unlike the fellow in the song, this ex-Oklahoman keeps on an even keel as he preserves the Pontiac-Oakland legacy.

Pontiac-Oakland Museum 205 N. Mill Street, Pontiac, IL 61764
www.PontiacOaklandMuseum.org

Love Me Fender:
The Cars of Elvis and More in Memphis

Presley Motors Automobile Museum at Graceland & Edge Motor Museum Memphis, Tennessee

There are two museums of interest to classic car fans in Memphis, Tennessee. The first, at Graceland, has created a new look at one of the biggest global stars in history, while the second is one of the newest car museums in America.

Riding with the King

Along with all his musical talent, deep down, Elvis Presley was a car guy. In fact, car museums across are America are sprinkled with Lincoln Continentals that Elvis gave out to close friends like candy on Halloween. The Presley Motors Automobile Museum at Graceland (completely overhauled in 2017) highlights a dozen of his cars, along with various other vehicles he rode, including motorcycles, boats, and even his favorite tractor.

In keeping with Presley's later flamboyant Vegas era, the cars are displayed on raised aluminum podiums under track spotlighting. Multiple screens show Elvis and friends driving the cars around Graceland, along with assorted clips from his movies.

The star of the collection is the hot pink 1955 Cadillac Fleetwood Series 60 he bought for his mother Gladys as a gift; the fact that she couldn't drive didn't deter him. The 1960 MG convertible in Chariot Red (who knew chariots had colors?) is the car Elvis drove around the exotic tropical locale in the film *Blue Hawaii*. He liked it so much that after filming wrapped, he purchased it for his collection but, in typical Presley style, gave it away a few years later to his secretary.

Presley was also a motorcycle enthusiast. Several of his bikes are on display including a custom red 1976 Harley-Davidson Electra-Glide with less than 1,000 miles on it; the red, white, and blue side reflector with "1976" emblazoned on it commemorated the nation's bicentennial. A hog of another stripe is a Harley-Davidson golf cart from the company's foray into sedate four-wheeled transportation.

In a tableau reminiscent of Rosebud from *Citizen Kane*, Presley's sled is also on display, a poignant reminder of both leading characters' lives. Another sad reminder of the end of Elvis's life is his beloved 1973 Stutz Blackhawk III. A photo next to the car shows him driving it through the gates of Graceland for the last time on August 16, 1977. Hours later he was found dead.

The automobile museum is one of the many exhibits at Graceland – to gain admission you must purchase a pass to the entire complex. Compared to visiting other car museums it's not a cheap ticket; plan on visiting the Graceland mansion and other exhibits on-site (which include his many gold records and a stunning array of his costumes) to get the most value from your experience. Overall, we found the visit to the second most visited home in America (after the White House) to be worthwhile – you can even stroll through the famous shag carpeted Jungle Room and refresh yourself with a peanut butter and banana sandwich (the King's favorite) at Gladys' Diner.

Life on the Edge

Lovers of both cars and Elvis have a second site to explore in Memphis, "The Edge" district near downtown. Anchored by the famous Sun Studio, where Presley and other musical greats such as Johnny Cash, B.B. King, and Roy Orbison recorded, the area is now home to the Edge Motor Museum. One of America's newest car museums opened in 2019, just 200 yards up the street from Sun Studio, providing an additional anchor to this hip neighborhood.

The Edge Motor Museum is a 20-car collection that focuses on American cars in the post-war era through 1974. Founded by local businessman Richard Vining, the museum features his own cars, along with those loaned by local car club members. Fittingly, the 1920s building was originally the home of Cherokee Motors, who designed, built, and sold their vehicles on the premises.

The renovation work is impressive, creating an internal ramp down to the auto showroom that reminds one of a mini version of the Guggenheim Museum in New York. Some of the cars that were in place for the grand opening included the 1949 Crosley Hotshot #19 that won the inaugural Sebring endurance race on New Year's Eve 1950, a 1954 Corvette, and a 1963 Avanti. These cars all fit into the first exhibition, called "American Speed." According to Vining, "Our goal is to show how the cars related to the economic, political, cultural, and technological eras in which they were built."

Many of the museum's visitors – a good chunk of whom are from overseas – stroll over after their Sun Studio visit. According to Vining, "We're finding that the deep knowledge of American vehicles internationally is very impressive."

Presley Motors Automobile Museum at Graceland 3765 Elvis Presley Blvd, Memphis, TN 38116 www.Graceland.com

Edge Motor Museum 645 Marshall Avenue, Memphis, TN 38103 www.EdgeMotorMuseum.com

HIGH PLAINS DRIFTERS

SPEEDWAY MOTORS MUSEUM OF AMERICAN SPEED Lincoln, Nebraska

Once early automobiles got produced in increasing numbers, it was inevitable that racing them would follow. That quest for competition and velocity is celebrated at the Speedway Motors Museum of American Speed in Lincoln, Nebraska. Touted as the "World's Largest Collection of Exotic Racing Engines & Vintage Speed Equipment," it was founded by Bill "Speedy" Smith and his wife Joyce in 1992. Long active in racing and hot rodding, the Smiths started Speedway Motors, the after-market performance parts company, four decades prior to the museum.

The collection occupies 150,000 square feet but is kept manageable for visitors as it is divided into more than 20 sections including Open Wheel, Land Speed, Dragsters, Le Mans, and more. Since Bill Smith was also a gearhead, there are almost as many exhibits devoted solely to engines. To round out the museum there are groupings of pedal cars, model taxis, racing-themed vintage pinball machines, and more. With more than 100 vehicles and several hundred engines, plus assorted racing paraphernalia, there's an incredible amount crammed into the three-story building, so allow plenty of time for a visit.

The first floor is a racing fan's dream that starts out with the Open Wheel era. Andy Granatelli owned the #57 STP racer painted in his team's signature Day-Glo red. (Anyone else have one of those ubiquitous STP stickers emblazoned on their high school notebooks?) Although it dropped out of the Indy 500 in 1969, later that summer it was the first across the finish line at Dover Downs while being driven by Art Pollard. By then its engine had been replaced with a naturally aspirated 318 cubic inch Plymouth; it became the first winner of an Indy series race in a Plymouth engine.

Between 1939 and 1947 (with a four-year gap for World War II) the #8 Blue Crown Spark Plug Special qualified for the Indy 500 on five separate occasions. The all-aluminum racer was the first to run at Indy with four-wheel disc brakes.

In the Dragsters section the 1953 #303 Bell Engine Roadster was a product of seat-of-the-pants homemade engineering by Californians Reid and Don Pate who, along with Bill Crissman, created a revolutionary rear-engine racer. The setup led to minimal wheel spin and fishtailing, giving it an advantage on drag tracks. The rear deck of the car is raised so visitors can view the Mercury Flathead engine that powered it.

Luxury speed is not left out with two cars capable of rapid street times: a 1948 Tucker #1024 and a 1930 Duesenberg Model J four-door convertible with a body by Murphy of California. The Duesy's DOHC I-8 engine could push the car to 116 mph.

The aerodynamic 1935 Miller-Ford is another Preston Tucker connection; the four-wheel independent suspension front-wheel-drive car was the product of a joint venture among Tucker, Harry Miller, and the Ford Motor Company. Around ten were designed and produced in an exceptionally short time frame of sixty days, while four raced at the 1935 Indy 500. Unfortunately, that compressed time frame showed at the track and none of them finished the race; this one completed 71 laps and ended up 24th in the standings.

The Land Speed section features Els Lohn's 1961 Eelco Wee Eel. The aerodynamic land torpedo reached 203 mph on a 4-cylinder engine.

Anyone who ever made plastic model cars in the 1960s and '70s is familiar with the iconic Red Baron. The Monogram kit designed by Tom Daniel was released in 1968 and became a huge best seller. The next year Chuck Miller of Styline Customs built a full-sized Red Baron that is on display here. The original plastic model sported a Mercedes-Benz Fokker airplane engine, but Miller chose a 1968 Pontiac overhead cam inline six for his Red Baron. Speaking of toys, 500 pedal cars are on display, the oldest of which dates to 1891. It didn't take long after cars were invented to get the tykes driving them.

While engines are displayed on pedestals throughout the museum, the Miller Room – featuring the output of Indy 500 legend Harry Miller – is a highlight. A 272 ci DOHC V-16 is one of only two V-16s he produced; it competed in the 1947 Indy 500. Miller's 1932 308 ci DOHC V-8 engine was placed in a four-wheel-drive racing car for the 1932 Indy 500.

A vestibule leading upstairs is decorated with hundreds of auto-themed record album covers including the likes of Richard Petty and the Roaring Sound of NASCAR. Vintage movie posters feature one from the original Gone in 60 Seconds film that premiered in 1974. I'd never heard of any of the stars, but there was a guest appearance by racecar driver Parnelli Jones. The tagline was "See 93 cars destroyed in the most incredible chase ever filmed."

The second floor is Ford heaven, with separate areas devoted to the Model T, Model A and B, and Flathead Ford V-8 engines. A real one-of-a-kind is the 5 millionth Ford produced (the engine number is 5,000,000) a 1931 Ford Model T Coupe.

Bill's wife Joyce was not to be denied her own motor-related collection, which in her case was yellow taxis. Unlike the Joni Mitchell song, Joyce's taxis are little, not big. The third floor of the museum sports a collection of model taxis, pedal cars, and even a taxi bumper car from an amusement park. At first this collection might seem at odds with a museum focused on racing and speed. But if you've ever been late for a flight, you'll know that the taxi – and driver – taking you to the airport were competing in a unique race on city streets to get you to the finish line.

Speedway Motors Museum of American Speed 599 Oakcreek Drive, Lincoln, NE 68528

www.MuseumOfAmericanSpeed.com

Stahls Automotive Foundation in Michigan

Stahls Automotive Foundation Chesterfield, Michigan

Stahls Automotive Foundation is one of the most fascinating car museums that you've never heard of. Tucked away in an office park just 35 miles northeast of downtown Detroit, it's a must-see sight for anyone visiting the Motor City. But it will take some planning; the museum is only open to the public on Tuesdays and the first Saturday of the month. It's worth the effort to see a display of more than 80 cars (out of a collection of more than 120) ranging from an 1899 De Dion-Bouton tricycle through a 1967 Pontiac GTO convertible.

The museum is the creation of local entrepreneur Ted Stahl. In 1990, Ted and his wife Mary purchased a 1930 Ford Model A Roadster Deluxe to restore with their kids. That one car led to another . . . and then another, and before he knew it, Ted owned an entire museum's worth of cars. His hobby is the public's gain as a remarkable collection is now on view.

Perhaps he was inspired by the family story behind the 1939 Ford Midget Racer in the lobby: a gift to William Clay Ford on his 14th birthday – the legal age to drive at the time – that was designed by his grandfather Henry and father Edsel. (I got a new horn for my bicycle for my 14th birthday.)

The cars are divided into seven categories: 1) Veteran Era; 2) Brass Era; 3) Vintage; 4) Pre-war; 5) Post-war; 6) Performance; and 7) Movie Cars. For those in your group who need a distraction while you spend hours poring over the cars, there's an incredible selection of antique Music Machines providing a vintage soundtrack to a visit. They range from a Wurlitzer theater organ to a massive Gaudin dance hall organ – it's so large that the four gold statues flanking the façade look downright Lilliputian even though they are nine feet tall.

The cars are laid out in rough chronological order starting around the turn-of-the-last century, with a corner devoted to General Motors co-founder William Durant, whom Stahl admired for his legendary resilience. Among the cars in "Durant Corner" is a 1910 Buick Model F sporting a two-cylinder engine that was mounted underneath the body, not the hood.

A rare 1904 Oldsmobile Model N "French Front" Touring runabout was so named for the front grille's rectangular shape, mimicking the cars coming out of France, rather than the iconic Olds curved dash. The Model N also boasted an Oldsmobile first – a steering wheel now replaced the tiller. A real oddity is the 1904 Cyklonette Trike; the three-wheeled German vehicle was a bit difficult to operate as the throttle, mixture, and ignition controls were all mounted on the tiller.

In a lesson for auto manufacturers over the years, the 1907 Pope-Toledo XV Touring was built in Connecticut without regard for whether there was enough demand for such a high-end vehicle (it cost the equivalent of $160,000 today). Within five years the company was bankrupt and only a handful of these prestigious cars survive.

The museum really shines with its collection of pre-World War II marques. The 1934 LaSalle Roadster Series 50 Model 350, designed by the legendary Harley Earl, was the only convertible produced by LaSalle that year. Seven years earlier General Motors had launched their Art and Color Section, which became influential in new vehicle design – this striking car was one of the results. The tall, slender grille was a nod to contemporary British land speed racers.

The 3.2-liter 6-cylinder engine on the 1936 Mercedes-Benz 320 convertible has its original matching numbers. One of the options on this model is "Autobahn Gearing," an overdrive setting provided by a separate gear lever on the floor. The 1936 Hudson Terraplane Deluxe Series 61 exhibits Art Deco styling that was aviation influenced – the first two Terraplanes went to Orville Wright and Amelia Earhart. The cream of the crop is the 1934 Duesenberg Model J that represents the pinnacle of American automotive excellence. It boasts its original straight-8 engine that put out 265 hp.

In the post-war era, a 1948 Tucker #1015 often faces off against a 1948 Tatra. With their three-headlight front grille and rear-engine configuration they look like kindred spirits. The 1954 Kaiser Darrin was an acquired taste. It features a revolutionary fiberglass body, "pursed lips" front grille and sliding (!) doors, which, over time, can be a chore to open and close.

The comparative post-war automotive stylings of the United States and Germany are rendered in stark contrast in a side-by-side display. A leviathan 1958 Ford Fairlane 500 Skyliner convertible with retractable hardtop is parked next to a diminutive 1958 Zundapp Janus that looks like it could fit in the trunk of the Ford. The Zundapp is often mistaken for an Isetta but, unlike that car, it has two doors – one opens the front, and one opens the rear, while the seat folds down to turn it into a camper. Despite that nifty feature, the car didn't sell enough units and the company went bankrupt.

For embarking on a road trip in style, a two-tone turquoise and white 1963 Volkswagen Type 2 23-window Super Deluxe Microbus met mid-century needs, particularly with a split-windscreen that opened to provide ventilation. It's trailing a rare 1967 Eriba Puck caravan in matching colors. Next to it is a canary yellow 1951 Kaiser Traveler saloon. The model earned its moniker by providing America's first hatchback car; the trunk lid and rear window hinged upwards from the top to provide easy access to storage and camping gear.

For transportation inclinations that are more nautical in nature, the German 1964 Amphicar 770 convertible, powered by a British Triumph Herald 4-cylinder engine, can ply the waves in style. Its top speeds were 7 mph on water and 70 mph on land, hence the 770 designation.

While many museums are of the "Don't Touch" variety, Stahls provides four cars where visitors can get behind the wheel for a photo opportunity, including a 1910 Ford Model T fire engine and, for a tight squeeze, a 1961 Isetta.

Stahls Automotive Foundation 56516 N. Bay Drive, Chesterfield, MI 48051
www.StahlsAuto.com

From Carriages to Coupes

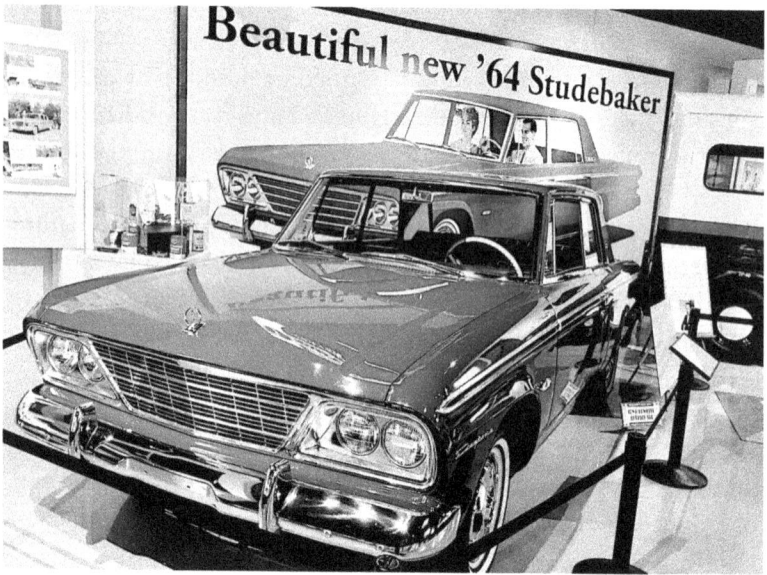

STUDEBAKER NATIONAL MUSEUM South Bend, Indiana

Motoring fans know Studebaker as a former manufacturer of cars with great repute. But the company's roots go back much farther: a 19th-century American pioneer crossing the Great Plains was likely driving a Studebaker-manufactured horse-drawn wagon, also known as a prairie schooner. The Studebaker National Museum honors the company's heritage in its former main manufacturing hub of South Bend, Indiana.

The original five Studebaker brothers were blacksmiths and wagon builders when they founded the company in 1852. (The company later paid homage to this heritage with the 1954-1955 Studebaker Conestoga station wagon.) In 1902, the company leapt into the newfangled automotive world, initially manufacturing electric powered cars and trucks. A total of 20 electric vehicles were produced that first year. However, within a decade they abandoned electric propulsion, and focused instead on gasoline-powered cars.

The company thrived during World War I. In 1914, the British War Office, in a reprise of orders they had placed with Studebaker during the Boer War, cabled in an initial order for 3,000 transport wagons. Although, in a step backwards technologically, they were only 2 to 4 horsepower because they were literally drawn by horses.

The museum sprawls over three floors, displaying a rotating assortment of about 70 vehicles drawn from the 120-vehicle collection. Permanent exhibits include the Presidential Carriage Collection and the Military Collection. Hearkening back to the company's roots, the Presidential Carriage Collection includes the Studebaker carriage that carried President Abraham Lincoln on his fateful journey to Ford's Theatre.

But most of the floor space is set aside for celebrating Studebaker's motoring heritage. The 1928 Studebaker Commander set endurance and speed records in Atlantic City, New Jersey when it was driven for 25,000 miles in 23,000 minutes, averaging 65 mph. Rarities include a top-of-the-line 1932 President St. Regis Brougham. One of only five in existence, it is distinguished by its oval headlights.

The 1933 Rockne is a vestige of a separate subsidiary set up within Studebaker called Rockne Motors after the legendary University of Notre Dame football coach Knute Rockne. (The university is also located in South Bend.) Unfortunately, Rockne died in a plane crash before the car was introduced and it was only in production for two years.

The wood-sided 1947 Champion Deluxe station wagon is a rarity. The model was dropped before production began so this prototype was discarded for years in the infield of the Studebaker Proving Ground test track. In poor condition, an 18-year restoration was completed in 2012.

During the 1950s Studebaker developed a reputation for unique styling, distinguishing the marque from its motoring counterparts.

The sleek European-looking 1953 Champion Starliner, designed by Robert Bourke, was heralded on the cover of *TIME* magazine, and showcased at New York City's Museum of Modern Art.

The 1950 Commander Starlight Coupe features the bullet nose that became Studebaker's signature for, alas, only two years. If this bullet nose looks familiar, you may have caught it in 1979's *The Muppet Movie* when it was driven by Kermit the Frog and Fozzie Bear on an epic road trip. In the film the car was operated by a hidden driver who was perched in the trunk and watched the road via a video monitor embedded in the bullet nose. Now, minus its distinctive paint job, the actual prop car used in the movie sits in the cellar of the museum in the Visible Storage System area.

Here, several dozen unusual vehicles that Studebaker produced over the years are on display, including a 1963 Truck Prototype that primarily used flat sheet metal and glass components to create an inexpensive, if somewhat boxy, small truck. The project was halted when Studebaker stopped all production at its South Bend plant that year. In 1936 Studebaker introduced the Ace, its first cab-forward delivery truck which increased maneuverability in tight urban settings.

The late 1950s and early 1960s brought some revolutionary concept cars and prototypes in the hope of positioning the company better for the future. The 1950s Astral looks like it was the inspiration for the bubble-top flying cars in *The Jetsons* cartoon show. The 1962 Notchback Prototype sedan was designed by Raymond Loewy and built by Pichon-Parat of Paris. Somewhat in competition with Loewy, designer Brooke Stevens came up with the aerodynamic 1962 Sceptre Prototype. With Sylvania tubular headlights and taillights that stretched from side to side it looks like it stepped out of the set of Moonraker. It was built by Sibona-Bassano in Turin, Italy.

One edgy design that did make it to the production line in the waning years of Studebaker was the Raymond Loewy-designed Avanti. Introduced in 1962, the four-seater sports car boasted a profile that was so quirky it was the favorite boyhood car of shock rocker Alice Cooper. According to Cooper, who now owns an Avanti, "People hated how the car looked but I liked it because it's got this asymmetrical body and was just the weirdest car. When it came out, I was 15 and I thought it was the coolest thing I'd ever seen in my life."

A 1963 Avanti #9 that is on view, powered by a 411 hp V8 motor, reached 170.81 mph at the Bonneville Salt Flats in 1963. While the name Avanti meant "forward" in Italian, it represented the finale of innovations by the proud Studebaker company.

The literal end of the line for Studebaker is represented by the 1964 Daytona Hardtop. It was the last US-built Studebaker (production continued in Canada through 1966) rolling off the line on the plant's final day in late 1963. It had been sold to a customer in Pennsylvania but the company switched the cars so they could hold onto this historic final vehicle. There are only 24 miles on the odometer.

Touch screens throughout the museum allow visitors to view even more information about Studebaker's motoring heritage.

Studebaker National Museum 201 Chapin Street, South Bend, IN 46601

StudebakerMuseum.org

Celebrating Classic Car Heritage
in America's Dairy State

Wisconsin Automotive Museum Hartford, Wisconsin

Hartford, Wisconsin is the former home of the Kissel Motor Car Company. Active from 1906 through 1931, it produced the alliteratively named Kissel Kar. Today, Hartford celebrates that heritage at the 115-vehicle Wisconsin Automotive Museum, which sprawls over 75,000 square feet on two floors as it pays tribute to Kissel, along with other Wisconsin marques, including Nash and Badger. The collection is rounded out mostly with other American cars, such as AMC (a Nash descendent), Pontiac, Studebaker, and Kaiser.

A Kollection of Kissels

For anyone with an interest in the somewhat obscure Kissel, this is the place to visit. Of the 27,000 Kissels produced, less than 150 survive today; nearly 20% of those – 27 – are on view here.

The Kissel Motor Car Company was founded by German immigrant Louis Kissel and his sons. After World War I, the Kissel Kar became simply "Kissel" as the moniker "Kar" was dropped due to its Germanic-sounding connotation. Louis' sons, George, and William, were engineers who determined that price shouldn't be an obstacle to producing the best quality automobile.

According to the March 1923 issue of *Automobile Dealer and Repairer-The Mechanical Motor Magazine*, "The Kissel Motor Car Company quickly established itself as a leader. From European cars, which had behind them more years of engineering history, Kissel took many of the best features and adapted them to American manufacturing methods."

At the museum, a 1912 Kissel 4-50 is in its original unrestored condition but still drives. It was the last Kissel with the steering wheel on the righthand side. It features carbide headlights and oil fueled side lamps.

Kissels were revered by forward-thinking motorists: famed aviator Amelia Earhart drove cross-country from California to Boston with her mother in 1923 in a Kissel Speedster. The pocket-sized 1923 Kissel Speedster on view reveals that spending so much time in the cramped quarters of an airplane taught Earhart to travel rather light.

The 1925 Kissel 75, with its 8-cylinder, 75 hp motor, was introduced at the National Automobile Show in New York. This example is unrestored and in all-original condition, except for its new top and tires. It is used as a reference template for other Kissel restorations.

A red 1926 Kissel 6-55 roadster shows off the gleaming finishing touch of 22 coats of paint, 8 more than its competitors, that was a trademark of Kissel. A pair of 1930 Kissel 8-95 White Eagles (a Touring and a Four Door Brougham) are two of only five known survivors from that year; there are no known remaining cars from the final model year of 1931, making these among the last Kissels ever manufactured.

A Stash of Nashes

The Nash Car Club of America also occupies space in the museum. Following a stint as the head of General Motors, Charles Nash founded the Nash Motor Company in 1916 by purchasing the Kenosha, Wisconsin based Thomas B. Jeffery Company that had started producing the Rambler automobile in 1897. (Thomas Jeffery was born in Devon, England and immigrated to Chicago. His son, Charles, who had inherited the company from him in 1910, sold it to Nash a year after surviving the sinking of the Lusitania.)

Nash leaned on his GM experience, and, with the slogan "give the customer more than he has paid for," rapidly increased the company's sales, becoming the 4th largest car company in the United States after GM, Ford, and Chrysler.

The 1918 Nash Quad truck (formerly known as the Jeffery Quad), known for its pioneering four-wheel driving, braking, and steering was a workhorse in World War I for the Allied forces. It was originally built to replace the four-mule team in the US Army.

A 1950 Nash Statesman Super Airflyte, in metallic Bermuda Blue paint with only 61 miles on the odometer, may be the lowest-mileage 72-year-old vehicle you'll ever see. It even sits on its original Goodyear Super Cushion tires. The purchaser, Frieda Braun, had every intention of learning to drive but never did. Every time she moved, she had the car towed to her new location. Subsequent owners decided not to drive the car either to preserve it as a unique automotive artifact.

The 1953 Nash-Healey Le Mans roadster is a British-American-Italian hybrid sports car (featuring Englishman Donald Healey of Austin-Healey fame) that combined an English Silverstone chassis mated with Nash running gear. The body style by Pinin Farina won first place at the 1953 Concours de Elegance in Paris. Only 506 were built, a much-modified version of which captured first in its class at the *24 Hours of Le Mans* in 1952.

In 1954, Nash merged with Hudson to form the American Motors Corporation. AMC cars have long had a quirky reputation. While most of my adolescent cohort yearned for sports cars like Camaros and Mustangs, those who thought "outside the box" wanted to be sitting behind the wheel of an AMC Javelin like the mustard yellow 1971 Javelin SST on display, which was produced in Kenosha, Wisconsin. The fastback coupe's base V8 engine pumped out 210 hp.

I have been to hundreds of car museums, yet this is the first time I've seen a prosaic 1979 AMC Concord on display. The compact station wagon was very popular due to the 1979 Oil Crisis and outsold all other AMC cars combined that year.

More American Rarities

Wisconsin is nicknamed the "Badger State" so naturally there was a Badger Motor Car Company. Founded in 1910, it only operated for two years producing 237 automobiles. Despite their success in hill climbs and endurance events, the company folded. The 1910 Badger Model B Touring Car is the only known survivor of the marque.

The Misty Yellow 1964 Mercury Comet Caliente is a real survivor. Floridian Rachel Veitch bought it new and drove it for the next 46 years, putting 563,000 miles on it. The only major work was an engine rebuild at half a million miles. For her automotive loyalty, in 2010 Veitch made an appearance on *The Tonight Show* with noted car buff Jay Leno.

Other attractions at the museum include a large-scale model car collection, a sprawling Lionel model train track and automotive collectibles.

Wisconsin Automotive Museum 147 N. Rural Street, Hartford, WI 53027 www.WisconsinAutoMuseum.com

WESTERN UNITED STATES

Clive Cussler Wrote the Book on Classic Cars

Cussler Museum Arvada, Colorado

Clive Cussler, the international best-selling author of thrillers featuring the classic-car-driving character Dirk Pitt, also collected cars himself. In 2006 he opened a museum near the mile-high city of Denver, Colorado. The 100+ car collection focuses on Concours d'Elegance quality 1920s and 1930s European and American luxury marques. Also featured are 1950s American convertibles and whatever else struck Cussler's fantasy at the time, often influenced by the plot of his latest page-turner.

Cussler's books often featured images of classic cars, either in a front cover illustration or making a cameo appearance in the author photo in back. In a novel twist, many of the cars in the museum are displayed with the book in which they appeared.

While Cussler passed away in early 2020, his legacy in the collector world lives on with his museum.

According to curator Keith Lowden, who has been with the museum since its opening and managed the collection long before that, "Mr. Cussler first started collecting cars in the mid-1970s. Back then he focused on European marques like Daimler, Bugatti, and Tatra. He was infatuated with coachbuilt cars."

Gradually he expanded his focus to the collection on view today. But no matter the country of origin or the type of vehicle, Cussler had a discerning eye for high-end cars and rare vehicles.

European Elegance

Luxury marques include a 1939 Bugatti Type 57C with a hood that looks long enough to land a fighter jet. Some of the cars were built for speed, like the 1929 4 ½-liter blower Bentley. It was a two-time winner of the Lyon International Vintage Race in France.

The 1951 Talbot-Lago T26 Grand Sport Record was owned by King Farouk, the last adult monarch of Egypt. The body by Ghia, known as a Pillarless Saloon, was so spacious that four people could comfortably fit in the front seat. Ghia took streamlining to an extreme as there are no bumpers and the skirted over wings swing out on hinges to change a tire. The 4.5-liter inline 6-cylinder engine is a descendent of the Talbot-Lago Grand Prix racing car.

That same year produced the 1951 Daimler DE36. It's part of a series of eight Daimlers produced from 1945 through 1953 that were known as the Green Goddess, although not all of them were green. According to the Jaguar Heritage trust, the sobriquet derives from the 1948 Earls Court Motor Show in London where a jade green D36 was a hit with the crowd.

The model here, in burgundy and gray, sports a straight eight 150-hp motor to push the 3-ton, 147-inch wheelbase behemoth. The fenders are so large they hold storage bins for tools and luggage.

Although three left-hand drive Green Goddesses were shipped to the United States, this one is a right-hand drive vehicle.

The 1921 Rolls-Royce Silver Ghost features a mammoth 7.4-liter engine. It's called an All Weather Cabriolet as it featured roll up windows. Other elegant vehicles include a 1925 Isotta Fraschini Tipo 8 roadster with storage for the top in the rear boattail. A later iteration, the 1929 Isotta Fraschini Tipo 8a SS Coupe, ranked as one of the most expensive Italian cars ever.

Cussler featured the pink raspberry colored 1936 Avions Voisin C-28 Ambassade in his book Sahara, where his hero Dirk Pitt drove it across the desert. Understandably, for the film version a replica was used. Other French marques include a 1948 Delahaye Type 135 convertible created by prominent coachbuilder Henri Chapron and a 1951 Delahaye Type 235, with coach built by Philippe Charbonneau, that competed in the 1954 Rallye Sablé-Solesmes.

The Czech-built 1947 Tatra Type 87 is an outlier in the collection. With its air-cooled rear engine and triple headlight configuration, it looks like a precursor to the Tucker of later cinematic fame.

American Abundance

A lime green 1918 Cadillac Type 57 Sports Phaeton with a 315 ci V8 has an impressive pedigree. The coach, with its swept back windshield, was built by a young designer named Harley Earl at his family business, Earl Automobile Works, in Los Angeles. The client was theatre mogul Flo Ziegfeld, who gave the car to his wife, actress Billie Burke, best known for her role in *The Wizard of Oz* as Glinda, Good Witch of the North.

The 1936 Duesenberg Model J-577 was one of the last 10 cars produced of this illustrious marque. Coach built by Rollston, the limousine differed from other 'Doozies' due to its landaulet body, where the rear top folded down over the passenger section. Showing only 70,444 miles, it's one of the most original Duesenbergs in existence. Only the leather over the rear top and the chauffeur's seat have been replaced.

The 1937 Pierce-Arrow Travelodge Trailer is a rarity. The Great Depression caused the Buffalo, New York company to grasp at any straw to maintain sales. Yet going into the RV business was an odd decision for an upscale car maker. The 16½ foot Model B camper sleeps 4 and could be ordered in an enamel paint color to match the tow car. Only twelve are known to survive. Here it's being towed by a 1936 Pierce-Arrow V12 Berline, making it the ritziest setup at the campground. The V12 put out 185 hp for a top speed of 110 mph. (One assumes that's without a camper attached.) Cussler's hero Dirk Pitt drove this combination in his novel *Inca Gold*.

A row of 1950s and '60s convertibles are colossal even by the land-yacht standards of their era of post-war exuberance. The 1957 Mercury Turnpike Cruiser Convertible was the flagship for the marque and sped around the Brickyard as that year's Indianapolis 500 pace car. All were painted in Sun Glitter yellow, while the fenders were adorned with gunsights that flashed in sync with the turn indicators. The 1958 Buick Series 700 Limited managed to achieve 300 hp despite its 2-½ ton heft.

The unitized body of the 1959 Lincoln Continental Mark IV stretched more than 19 feet on a 131-inch wheelbase. It needed a 430 cubic inch engine to generate 350 horsepower. It's beautifully restored to its original turquoise color. The 1960 Imperial Crown Convertible was a separate luxury marque offered by Chrysler. The driver's seat was elevated from the passenger's and swiveled for easy of entry and exit. Now that's luxurious.

The Cussler Museum is a worthwhile visit that showcases a collection of elegant automobiles that the author created from a lasting literary legacy.

Cussler Museum 14959 W. 69th Avenue, Arvada, CO 80007
www.CusslerMuseum.com

Note: The museum is typically open on select days between April and September. Check the website for their schedule.

Franklins in the Desert

Franklin Auto Museum Tucson, Arizona

If you can find the unassuming Franklin Auto Museum, congratulations are in order. It's tucked away in a residential neighborhood north of downtown Tucson, Arizona that opted not to have their streets paved. So, plan to drive on some sandy roads dodging cacti for a few blocks before you arrive at the museum's three adobe buildings, which is really part of the fun when viewing such a fine assemblage of pre-World War II cars.

This 27-car collection of Franklin automobiles grew out of the passion of one man, car restorer Thomas Hubbard. (Legendary collector Bill Harrah was among his resto clients.) He purchased his first Franklin in 1950 and never stopped. His love affair with Franklins began earlier at age eight when his family acquired a brand new 1933 model, although he soon had to defend his love of Franklins to his friends. Bill, a guide at the museum who as a child used to hang around helping Hubbard's auto restorations, recalls Hubbard saying, "They'd rib me about the car. I had to explain to my friends, why if the car was so good, they didn't make them anymore." Hubbard died in 1993 but the foundation he established funds the museum and its continued acquisition of cars. It recently even bought a 1905 Franklin Model A Runabout with a rare rear-entry *tonneau*.

Franklins were produced in Syracuse, New York from 1902 through 1934 under the guidance of engineer John Wilkinson and businessman Herbert H. Franklin, whose personal motto was "It can be done." He also founded the world's first machine die-casting business.

All the Franklins were air-cooled. Because air-cooling removed the need for a bulky radiator, Franklin cars took on some unusual front-end shapes including barrel hoods, shovels, and horse collars. Pricewise they ran just under a Cadillac; although over 150,000 Franklins were produced, only about 3,500 survive today.

There are three rooms' worth of autos here. Because early cars required constant maintenance, the 1918 Franklin Model B Touring came with tool kits; the originals are cleverly hidden inside the front doors, with extra spark plugs to boot. See if you can find the handy (and surprisingly small) golf bag on the 1929 Franklin Convertible Coupe. In a sign of the times, with Charles Lindbergh having crossed the Atlantic Ocean (with an air-cooled engine) just two years before, an airplane logo was placed on the rear bumper to symbolize the car's "airplane-type" engine; further increasing its sportiness factor.

It's not all Franklins here though. In an outbuilding there are several other marques, including a 1909 REO Touring, which was the first car Thomas Hubbard restored. A 1929/1930/1931 Franklin Model 153 is unique because it was company founder Herbert Franklin's personal vehicle. The reason it has so many model years attributed to it was that he brought it into the shop annually to update it to the current model year.

A one-off 1931 Franklin Model 153 Sport Phaeton was custom ordered by 21-year-old Stillman F. Kelley, II for his honeymoon. Despite the Great Depression raging, Kelley paid $6,500 for this beauty, and may have survived the financial downturn better than Franklin. The automaker had leveraged his company for growth that didn't materialize and was unable to shoulder the increased debt burden, declaring bankruptcy in 1934. The aircraft engine division survived but, in an odd twist, was bought in 1947 by Preston Tucker to produce engines for the Tucker 48.

A visit to the museum offers the opportunity to take in a bit of authentic roadside Americana located nearby. Anyone who loves road trips is aware of the Muffler Man statues that sprinkle the heartland. These distinctive, 20-foot-tall fiberglass figures were mostly erected in the 1960s to lure visitors to various shops and attractions. They were cleverly designed so the statue could hold an object related to the business they were promoting.

They came to be known as "Muffler Men," regardless of what they held, because so many of them ended up holding mufflers to promote service stations. One of these icons of mid-century advertising presides over an intersection in Tucson, just two miles southwest of the Franklin Auto Museum. The circa-1964 fiberglass giant at the corner of N. Stone Avenue and E. Glenn Street is one of the earliest "Muffler Man" statues. This one's dressed up as Paul Bunyan holding an axe, yet it's still auto related, as it stands in the parking lot of Don's Hot Rod Shop at 2811 N. Stone Avenue, Tucson, AZ 85705.

Franklin Auto Museum 1405 E. Kleindale Road, Tucson, AZ 85719 (Entrance is at 3420 North Vine Avenue.)
www.FranklinMuseum.org

Note: Due to the summer heat in Tucson, the museum is usually only open from mid-October through Memorial Day.

A Double Dose of LeMays

LeMay Family Collection & LeMay-America's Car Museum
Tacoma, Washington

It's confusing but there are two incredible car museums with "LeMay" in their title in Tacoma, Washington. The original LeMay is the LeMay Family Collection. The later one is called LeMay – America's Car Museum. Despite the similarity of their names the museums are two separate entities. You with me so far?

LeMay Family Collection

The sprawling LeMay Family Collection is the legacy of entrepreneur Harold LeMay and his wife Nancy. The World War II veteran returned to his hometown of Tacoma after the war and started a rubbish hauling company that became one of the largest in the country.

During his trash hauling trips he'd come across abandoned cars and started collecting them. Once people knew of his interest, they brought them to his junkyard. He also bought a lot of used cars with a fondness for Chevy convertibles like the one he owned before he went off to war.

Eventually LeMay amassed a whopping collection of 3,000 vehicles that earned him a mention in the Guinness Book of Records as the world's "Largest Antique and Vintage Vehicle Collection. (Although, the majority are no longer trash finds.)

More than 500 vehicles occupy every nook and cranny – including the rifle range and pool area – of the former Marymount Military Academy; in some areas they are stacked three high. The museum includes a nice balance of unique vehicles along with many daily drivers, lending a nostalgic touch to a visit here to see cars you remember from your youth.

It's difficult to even write about the breadth of the collection. In one corner, practically within arm's length of each other are a 1923 Dodge Brothers delivery van, 1926 Pierce-Arrow Model 80 roadster, 1939 American Bantam roadster, 1954 Buick Roadmaster 76C, and a 1954 Kaiser Darrin KF-161 roadster. Designed by Howard "Dutch" Darrin, the latter features iconic sliding doors.

The museum owns a 1948 Tucker, #1007, which they refer to as "the one that got away" from the acquisitive Harold LeMay. The family purchased it after his death.

There's also an eclectic bunch of European cars including an Austrian 1935 Steyr 120 Super convertible, an Australian built 1953 Ford Anglia, left-hand drive 1959 Morris Minor, and a 1960 Fiat Abarth Zagato.

Consider visiting Tacoma on the last Sunday in August, when the LeMay Family Collection offers special tours of the LeMay home, where yet another 200 vehicles are on display. During my most recent visit, they stated they're still adding to the collection.

As I was strolling around the museum grounds, I ran into an overall-clad man doing some repairs on a flagpole. We chatted about the stunning collection of cars when he volunteered about LeMay,

"He was a tinkerer. He didn't have a lot of time to work on cars, but he knew what he had to do to get them running." I later found out that I had been speaking to one of LeMay's sons, Doug LeMay. The LeMay Family Collection really is a hands-on family affair.

LeMay – America's Car Museum

Across town, LeMay - America's Car Museum, while not as big as the LeMay Family Collection, is no slouch as it holds more than 250 vehicles; much of the collection was donated by LeMay himself. Despite the similarities in their name, the museums are separate entities.

Where the sprawling LeMay Family Collection is more homespun as it fills out every nook and cranny of the former school, the Lemay - America's Car Museum building, with its giant silver caterpillar shape, looks like something that landed in Tacoma from a galaxy far far away.

The main area on the upper level, with arching wooden walls and ceiling, is the size of an airplane hangar and is the setting for temporary exhibits. A recent display included "Reclaimed Rust," the collection of Metallica member James Hetfield. Then visitors descend sloping ramps to see the rest of the museum. The ramps and exposed ductwork ceilings give it the feel of an upscale parking garage catering only to classic cars.

Some of the cars are arranged thematically (like Route 66) while others are one-offs like the 1917 Crane Simplex Model 5 that is one of only 40 cars the company built that year and was formerly owned by oil magnate John D. Rockefeller, Jr.

One of the crown jewels is a 1927 LaSalle by legendary designer Harley Earl for General Motors that according to the Henry Ford Museum archives was "the first mass-production car to be consciously stylized." The placard on the LaSalle says that Hemmings Motor News selected it as one the top 100 collector cars of all time.

A similar plaque adorns the 1937 Cord 812 Winchester. Designed by Gordon Buehring, it's renowned for its distinctive coffin nose and retractable headlights. It also featured front-wheel drive.

Other pre-war American cars include a 1939 American Bantam Roadster stylized by future Tucker designer Alex Tremulis and a 1939 Crosley convertible that was introduced as "The Car of Tomorrow" at the 1939 World's Fair in New York. Car dealers weren't buying that description though so the air-cooled 12 hp roadster ended up being sold in Macy's and Bamberger's department stores along with Crosley radios and appliances.

The 1948 Ford Super Deluxe Station Woodie Wagon in original Glade Green was one of the last of the wood bodied cars. They were just too expensive to produce. Its sheer beauty shows people of my generation, who grew up with station wagons with imitation wood decals on the side, what we missed.

A blue 1966 Buick Skylark Gran Sport with a white hardtop sits under a sign that says This Car's My Favorite. The Wildcat 401 cubic inch engine was designed to pull performance minded buyers away from the popular Mustang and GTO.

According to our guide, "Money was not what Harold LeMay was about. He was a simple man who wanted to share history." In that, he succeeded immensely.

LeMay Family Collection 325 152nd Street, Tacoma, WA 98445
www.LeMayMarymount.org

LeMay – America's Car Museum 702 East D Street, Tacoma, WA 98421
www.LeMayMuseum.org

California Dreamin': Two Museums Inspire Very Different Automotive Fantasies

Mullin Automotive Museum & Murphy Auto Museum
Oxnard, California

The Mullin Automotive Museum and Murphy Auto Museum are both located in Oxnard, California, an oceanfront community 60 miles northwest of Los Angeles. However, there the similarity ends. In atmosphere and feel the two museums are light years apart.

The Mullin showcases French design in a sleek bi-level 65-car display (culled from a larger collection) of primarily Art Deco automobiles that deserve to sit on the pedestals that a few of them occupy. The Murphy is a more homespun collection that hearkens back to enthusiastic local car buffs who collect daily drivers, along with station wagons and vintage RVs. You shouldn't see one without seeing the other as they convey a wide swath of classic American and European cars, and the dreams associated with them.

Dreams of Design Excellence

The term "rolling sculpture" is often bandied about in the car world, but pre-war Bugattis really live up to that moniker. Their presence at the Mullin gives the museum the look of a high-end sculpture garden. While several of the automobiles here are literally placed on a pedestal, pride-of-place goes to the 1936 Bugatti Type 57SC Atlantic. The car is, to many, the most beautiful looking car of all time, which is why it's been called the "Mona Lisa" of the classic car world. It was designed by Ettore Bugatti's first son, Jean. Fashioned out of aluminum, the signature rivets on the dorsal fins are a design element left over from an earlier iteration. The other survivor of this rare vehicle is owned by Ralph Lauren.

The hood is lifted on a 1930 Bugatti Type 46 cabriolet to reveal the detailed machining on the engine block – it was so precise that no sealing gaskets were needed. A swept-back deep red 1939 Delahaye Type 165 debuted at the 1939 New York World's Fair (with no engine) while a 1951 Delahaye Type 23S cabriolet was first seen at the 1951 Paris Auto Salon.

However, it's not just high-end design at the Mullin; enduring French styling is on display with a Citroën exhibit. At first glance the 1990 Citroën 2CV6 looks like a car from the '50s; it was near the end of the line for a popular French daily driver that sold more than 3.8 million units from 1949 through 1991. A "sister" vehicle is the 1960 Citroën 2CV Camionette; a (very) small truck that was introduced in 1948 as a post-war replacement for rural French farmers who were still using horses and wagons. Other items in the collection include period furniture and paintings crafted by members of the artistically gifted Bugatti family.

One of the most unusual stories of any car in a museum anywhere is that of the 1925 Bugatti Type 22 Brescia Roadster. After a complicated history the vehicle was seized by Swiss authorities in the 1930s due to an unpaid tax bill; they later were forced to destroy it and did so by pushing it into Lake Maggiore. It was discovered by divers in 1967 at the bottom of the lake, 173 feet below the surface, and was eventually recovered in 2009. It now rests in its as-found condition at the Mullin alongside a life-size photo of its appearance under the lake.

You'll have to time your visit to the Mullin carefully. It is only open to the public on select Saturdays, but semi-private visits are also available on Tuesdays and Thursdays by reservation.

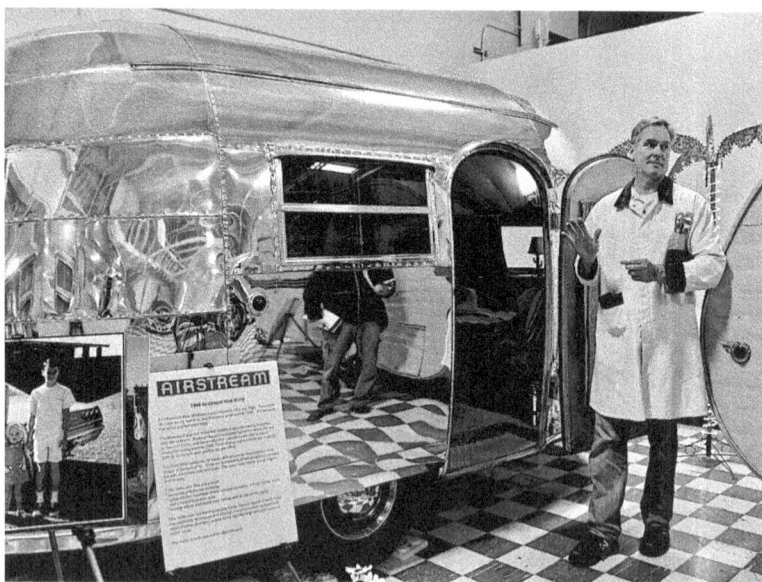

Dreams of Youth and Family Vacations at the Murphy

From the Mullin it's less than two miles to the Murphy Auto Museum. There you may be greeted by Executive Director David Neel wearing a white Studebaker mechanic's long coat, looking like he just stepped off the set of The Great Race after repairing Tony Curtis' Leslie Special.

Around 50 cars are usually on display. A few are owned by the museum; the rest are on short-term loan from private collectors who donate different vehicles each month. Accordingly, the collection is somewhat eclectic, ranging from a 1910 Los Angeles-built Duro to a 1956 Lincoln Capri to a 1964 Jeep Wagoneer. A wood-grained 1968 Chrysler Newport Town & Country station wagon is something not often found in museums and it's nostalgic to see daily drivers from our youth.

Most car museums don't focus on campers and station wagons so it's a joy to see these icons of mid-century American road trips featured here. The gregarious Neel says, "My family tent-camped when we were smaller, but I always loved looking at the Airstreams and Shastas and Nomads. That's when the seeds were planted."

One of his favorites is the 1960 Holiday House. The "Holy Grail" of campers was developed by the Harry & David Company (of Christmastime mail-order fruit basket fame) to give their employees something to do in the off-season. Due to high prices less than 200 were produced and, despite their good looks, they didn't catch on. Other campers include an iconic 1948 Airstream Wee Wind and the only known example of a 1956 New Moon Car Top Camper that fits on *top* of a station wagon. Camping and fishing enthusiasts will enjoy a fiberglass 1962 Trailorboat – (that is the correct spelling) and just like it sounds it is part tear drop trailer and part boat that fits snugly on top.

It's surprising that Neel collects vintage campers – at 6'6" he barely fits into some of them – but he has field tested them all. He exclaims, "It's hard for me to squeeze into Corvettes and low ceiling trailers but I can sure fit in wagons and pickups. I love them!" A huge assortment of vintage camping memorabilia – exhibited both inside and outside the trailers – completes the tableau. Neel also enjoyed playing with metal Tonka trucks as a child and, one suspects, he still does, so there are plenty of those scattered around the premises as well.

For something completely different the museum has a pair of Studebaker R2 Avantis from 1963 and 1964. The 1963 Studebaker Wagonaire Daytona had an intractable problem: its retractable rear roof leaked, impacting sales and leading to its eventual demise.

The Mullin Automotive Museum and the Murphy Auto Museum provide enough interesting things to keep even the most jaded classic car buff happy. So, hop in the car, pop The Mamas and the Papas into the tape deck, and head up the coast to do some *California Dreamin'*.

Mullin Automotive Museum 1421 Emerson Avenue, Oxnard, CA 93033
www.MullinAutomotiveMuseum.com

Murphy Auto Museum 1930 Eastman Avenue, Oxnard, CA 93030
www.MurphyAutoMuseum.org

CLASSICS JACKPOT: TWO NEVADA MUSEUMS OFFER A DIVERSION FROM CASINOS

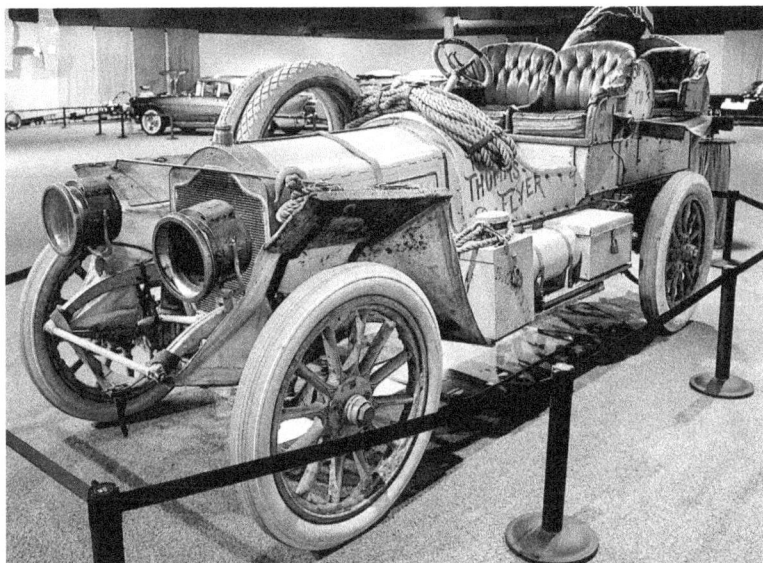

NATIONAL AUTOMOBILE MUSEUM: THE HARRAH COLLECTION Reno, NV & **SHELBY HERITAGE CENTER** Las Vegas, Nevada

The seven-hour drive from Reno to Las Vegas provides two interesting car museums at either end – the National Automobile Museum: Harrah Collection in Reno and the Shelby Heritage Center in Las Vegas – along with a side trip to a truly quirky automotive site: The International Car Forest of the Last Church, in the former mining town of Goldfield. As the name indicates, it's a bit "out there" – both metaphorically and geographically.

Start your Nevada sojourn in Reno at the National Automobile Museum. The 24-karat gold-plated DeLorean sitting in the lobby, one of two built for an American Express gold card promotion, immediately implies a touch of glitz. The 200-car collection that ranges back to an Ohio-built 1892 Philion steam car is largely comprised of vehicles that were once owned by casino magnate William "Bill" Harrah.

Harrah first started collecting in 1948 with the purchase of a 1911 Maxwell Runabout. From this small step he amassed one of the largest private collections in the world. When he died in 1978 many of them were sold off, but the nucleus of the collection survives at the museum – including that first Maxwell.

The stage is set with mock street scenes from the 1900s, 1930s, and 1950s. Here the cars are arrayed as if they were just out for a shopping trip in town. You'll see cars at the National Automobile Museum that you won't see elsewhere. What's so special about the 1914 Fiat Seven Passenger Touring? It is one of two known survivors that were built in upstate New York as part of the Italian automaker's attempt to increase its share of the American market.

The museum really shines with its select assortment of cars from between the two world wars. There are several one-of-a-kind prototypes, like the innovative 1925 Julian Sport Coupe with its rear-mounted, radial design engine. In keeping with the bling of the gold DeLorean parked in the lobby, the body of a 1921 Rolls-Royce is fabricated from solid copper sheets.

Perhaps the coolest car here is the 1937 Airomobile; this one-off was produced in Rochester, New York by former workers from the Franklin Automobile Company. While the aerodynamically sleek three-wheeled vehicle with a mermaid tale wouldn't look out of place in a Jetsons cartoon, it didn't catch on with the public. Its cool quotient will have to compete with the 1938 Phantom Corsair, an experimental six-passenger coupe that, with its elongated black hood, looks like a prototype of the George Clooney-era Batmobile.

Probably the most significant car in the collection is the 1907 Thomas Flyer. Listed on the National Historic Vehicle Register, it won the 1908 New York to Paris (by way of Siberia) automobile race. Harrah restored the car in the 1950s with assistance from George Schuster, the driver during that race. In fact, there are so many primo cars here that a 1948 Tucker #1032 almost gets lost in the shuffle, along with John Wayne's 1953 Corvette that was the 51st off the assembly line.

Las Vegas provides a treat for fans of Carroll Shelby at the Shelby Heritage Center, which is located inside the Shelby American manufacturing facility. Classic Cobras and continuation cars based on original chassis are lined up in rows, and you can also observe the shop floor where new models are being created for some lucky car buffs. Be careful though: if you just hit it big at one of the casinos, it might be tempting to drive away in one. Also included is a massive gift shop featuring various Shelby branded clothing and paraphernalia.

National Automobile Museum 1 Museum Dr. Reno, NV 89501
www.AutoMuseum.org

Shelby Heritage Center 6405 Ensworth Street, Las Vegas, NV 89119
www.Shelby.com_

About 250 miles southeast of Reno (and 185 miles northwest of Las Vegas), you'll run into the Goldfield Art Car Park and International Car Forest of the Last Church in Goldfield. This was once a town full of riches anchored by a mammoth gold mine.

For more than 20 years the town has been known for its heavily decorated "Art Cars" that are influenced by the Art Car Movement. From what I can determine, that involves sticking everything you can think of, including the kitchen sink in some cases, onto a vehicle. The flamboyantly decorated cars now reside along Highway 95, the main drag through town, and are collectively known as the Goldfield Art Car Park.

The International Car Forest of the Last Church is located on the outskirts of town. Here you'll find more than twenty vehicles plunked headfirst into the ground, most of them decorated with fanciful murals: think of the orderly row of tail-finned Caddys at Cadillac Ranch in Texas run amok.

It's easy to drive by and miss the entrance (look for the nearly vertical school bus perched precariously atop a ridge) that's located just south of town on Crystal Avenue. The dirt road rollercoasters a little bit, but it's worth the effort.

To Live and Drive in LA

PETERSEN AUTOMOTIVE MUSEUM Los Angeles, California

The Petersen Automotive Museum, with its popular dioramas of cars depicted in Los Angeles street scenes, has been a popular Los Angeles attraction ever since it opened in 1994. So, a few eyebrows were raised when the museum reopened in 2015 following a $125 million renovation to both the interior and exterior. Gone were the dioramas, replaced by sleek interior displays, all encased in a building wrapped with slithery stainless-steel ribbons. The Petersen had shifted from "reverse" to "drive" and hit the gas full throttle.

Shortly after the museum reopened, Leslie Kendall, the museum's Chief Historian told me, "We got some grief about removing the dioramas from people who loved them, but the reality is that museums have to continue to adapt and change." I must admit that I was one of those who liked how the dioramas evoked old Los

Angeles and wondered if the museum's new design could still do justice to automotive history.

I finally got my answer during my first post-renovation visit. Out on Wilshire Boulevard, the museum's controversial new shimmery skin declares to visitors that there's something special worth seeing inside. My initial impression inside was of the massive crowds on a Sunday afternoon that were more akin to what I'd expect wandering the galleries of the Louvre or the Smithsonian National Air and Space Museum, something not normally seen at a car museum.

I didn't miss the old Los Angeles street scenes; they would have looked a bit musty and dusty among the new displays. Noteworthy cars are spaced with plenty of room to walk all the way around them – the museum resisted the urge to jam in as many cars as possible – so visitors can truly appreciate their design from all angles. The effect is of a high-end art gallery.

Visitors begin on the third floor, where the theme is "History." The "Why We Love the Automobile" exhibit pays homage to automotive heritage. The 1900 Smith Runabout, with a two-cylinder air-cooled engine that cranks out an estimated 5 horsepower, is the oldest surviving gasoline powered vehicle built in Los Angeles. Notice the curved stanchions protruding from the headlight posts that were attachment points for a horse harness in the event the vehicle had to be towed.

Nearby is a real beauty: a 1959 Chevrolet Corvette Italia designed by coachwork builder Sergio Scaglietti, famous for his work with Ferrari. In conjunction with Carroll Shelby, Gary Laughlin, and Jim Hall he built three of these to combine the sexy stylings of a European sports car with the reliability of an American engine and chassis. General Motors eventually nixed the project and Shelby went on to fame teaming up with another American car manufacturer.

"Dream Cars: History of the Future" shows what mid-century designers could come up with when they let their imaginations run wild. A sleek 1953 Dodge Storm Z-250 by Bertone had two interchangeable bodies, one which was ultralightweight fiberglass to convert it for racing. The 1954 Plymouth Explorer by Ghia was another Chrysler/Italian partnership. The luxe interior includes fitted luggage and concealed radio controls.

The "Hollywood Gallery" highlights famous cars from film and television. A 1966 Ford Thunderbird was used for filming close-up shots – note the missing side view mirrors that would reflect the cameras – in *Thelma & Louise*. (Spoiler alert: This was not the car that soared into the Grand Canyon at the movie's end.) Cars rotate in and out of this section frequently, like the 1979 Volkswagen Transporter from *Little Miss Sunshine* or the 1958 Plymouth Fury from Stephen King's *Christine*. Unfortunately, Walter White's Pontiac Aztek from *Breaking Bad* was not on display during my visit, though whatever is missing is usually available on the Vault Tour.

The second floor, devoted to "Industry," offers a taste of the future of automotive design. In the Mullin Design Studio in the Art Center College of Design, undergraduate students actively sketch out plans for what we'll drive in a decade. According to Shijie, a third-year student from China, "We're here at the museum to let people know about the school and our design capability."

Across the hall, the *Cars* Mechanical Institute encourages would-be designers. In this family-friendly area, children can practice their art skills drawing cars, learn about the history of the automobile and race toy cars on a racetrack. It's a great place to introduce the next generation of car buffs to the hobby.

Other exhibits on the 2nd floor include Alternative Power, ranging from a 1915 Detroit Electric to a 1996 GM EV1; Hot Rods and Customs, High Performance Road Cars, and Motorsports. Museum founder Robert Petersen's career as a publisher is referenced in a wall of giant magazine covers including *Hot Rod* and *Motor Trend*. Much of the 1st floor is set aside for special exhibits that change throughout the year.

About 250 cars that belong to the museum that are not on display during your visit can usually be seen in the Vault. Guided Vault Tours require a separate ticket, but for completists who like to see everything, it's worth it. Since cars rotate in and out between the Vault and the main floors, you may need to take the Vault Tour to see a specific vehicle like the Ferrari that Tom Selleck drove in *Magnum, P.I.*

Overall, the Petersen Automotive Museum has been updated for the 21st century and the frequently changing exhibits encourage return visits. Judging by the large crowds, this new approach is popular, and provides hope for the future of the classic car hobby.

Petersen Automotive Museum 6060 Wilshire Blvd, Los Angeles, CA 90036

www.Petersen.org

Rambling Man:
The Joys of AMC Cars and More in Colorado

Rambler Ranch Elizabeth, Colorado

After snaking for miles through the rolling conifer carpeted foothills southeast of Denver, arriving at Rambler Ranch is a bit like discovering the mythical Scottish Highlands village that only came to life every 100 years in the musical Brigadoon. Collector Terry Gale has created a retro wonderland devoted to the cars of Rambler, Nash, and AMC and their associated memorabilia. More than 200 cars sprawl across a half dozen buildings, while another 600 vehicles (Gale has lost count) sit in the meadows out back.

According to the affable Gale, "The boneyard cars are parts cars and future projects. I bought them to save them from going to the crusher. This all started with rescuing my dad's 1954 Nash Ambassador. Dad bought it for 50 bucks in the early '70s in Utah and drove it for a few years until the oil pump went out at 120,000 miles. After it sat in a field for 18 years my brother said it was going to be hauled to the junkyard. Did I want it? After restoring the Nash, and seeing the positive reaction I had at car shows, I started collecting Nashes and had 30 cars by 1992. I opened the collection to the public a few years later."

Although the focus is on Rambler, Nash, and AMC, with a collection this large there are bound to be others who caught Gale's eye and, of course, there are. Gale continues, "We have 61 makers other than Nash/AMC," so don't be surprised to see the occasional Bricklin, Wolseley or Yugo lurking in the wings.

Gale usually starts a tour in the Nash building where he hops on a Segway and glides among the vehicles while passing original highway billboard advertisements. One of the rarest cars here is a 1955 Nash Ambassador prototype built in Italy and designed by Pininfarina. Bought from a collector in Pennsylvania, it retains its "1 OF 1" Pennsylvania license plate.

While most of my adolescent peers yearned for sports cars like Camaros and Mustangs, those of us who thought "outside the box" (okay, we were considered oddballs) wanted to be sitting behind the wheel of an AMC Javelin. So, I looked forward to the AMC building where more than 150 AMC cars from 1958 through 1988 are on display.

The interior is as vast as a hockey arena and boasts a major "wow" factor. The rows of cars go on for such a distance that it looks like the massive government warehouse at the end of *Raiders of the Lost Ark*.

So many are in groovy 1970s psychedelic shades like Mellow Yellow and Grasshopper Green I was surprised there isn't a giant mirror ball presiding over the gathering as I relived my disco era high school parking lot.

The bulk of the cars are those you wouldn't find in most museums, certainly not in the numbers displayed here. When was the last time you saw multiple Pacers parked in a row? Among them, a 1975

Pacer gleams in Metallic Aztec Copper, providing a counterpoint to the 1979 Pacer in a refined Wedgewood Blue.

A 1976 AMC Hornet, with only 2,600 miles, is liveried in a green Limefire exterior with a très chic brown plaid interior. A 1967 AMC Ambassador is right-hand drive since it was one of three thousand built as a mail delivery vehicle.

A 1981 Concord was 1 of about 200 aftermarket convertible conversions called the Sundancer that were created by the Fort Lauderdale, Florida based Griffith Company. An October 2018 copy of *Hemmings Classic Car* tucked under the wiper blades reveals it to be a former cover model for that magazine along with its stable mate, a converted 1981 Eagle Sundancer that Gale also owns.

A real rarity is seeing the complete line of 1967 Rambler Rebel regional station wagons – Briarcliff, Westerner, and Mariner – in one place. Marketed as a 1967 ½ surprise, they were sold in limited quantities in specific parts of the country. They also displayed a patriotic red, white, and blue motif in their exterior colors when lined up side by side. The Briarcliff is Matador Red, with simulated black grain leather side panels; the ranch-themed Westerner came in Frost White with simulated leather panels on the sides; while the Mariner, which was marketed to coastal cities, is Barbados Blue and distinguished by its simulated bleached teakwood planking and nautical motifs.

Other models that are just a dim memory from my youth include a 1967 AMC Marlin with the cool hood ornament of a Marlin jumping out of the water, a 1976 AMC Hornet, and a 1980 AMC Concord with vinyl rear roof and standard Ziebart factory rust protection.

Gales says, "AMC cars aren't expensive to collect, except for the Javelin." Despite that, he has managed to compile a handful including a 1968, 1969, 1974, and a 1969 AMX.

Since the place is named Rambler Ranch, there are several of those too including a 1958 Rambler Custom with original interior and a 1961 Rambler American. A brochure features Mitt's dad, AMC President George Romney, who touts the latter as the "New World

Standard of Basic Excellence!" due to several features including its exclusive Ceramic-Armored muffler and tail pipe and Deep-Dip rustproofing.

Of course, there's also a 1974 Gremlin, no description necessary.

The AMC Information Center overflows with hundreds of manuals, paint color and upholstery books, and more ephemera from the brand.

The Brand X building houses cars that don't fit neatly into the themed buildings. That's where you'll find beauties like a 1961 Studebaker Lark VIII in rare Flamingo Pink; an early aughts single-passenger Corbin Sparrow electric car that looks like it was designed by Salvador Dali drawing an egg (they made an appearance in an Austin Powers movie); and a 1984 Dodge 600 woodie convertible prototype that was one of two displayed at automobile shows across America.

A 1970 Jeep Hurst Jeepster Commando with a V8 is 1 of about 100 built that were planned to be part of a high-performance Hurst badged line. They came in Champagne White with red and blue striping that made it look a bit like a mail delivery vehicle. It's not in the AMC building because it was started when Jeep was owned by Kaiser.

Terry is so into all things Nash/AMC that he even devotes a building to Kelvinator appliances. (In 1937 Nash merged with Kelvinator, then in 1954 they merged with Hudson to form the American Motors Corporation.) There's also a recreated 1930s Sinclair service station that houses the souvenir shop and ice cream parlor.

Although tours are only offered on weekends, it seems like Gale is often up for a visit so contact him through the website to check on availabilies.

Rambler Ranch 36370 Forest Trail, Elizabeth, CO 80107
www.RamblerRanch.com

ROUTE 66 ELECTRIC VEHICLE MUSEUM Kingman, Arizona

One of the more recent additions of interest to car buffs road-tripping along the "Mother Road" is the Route 66 Electric Vehicle Museum in Kingman, Arizona. It's housed in the circa 1907 brick Powerhouse Building that, before the construction of nearby Hoover dam, provided electricity to the region via oil-fired steam-driven generators. The museum opened in 2014 and is billed as the only museum in the world devoted to electric vehicles.

Both former and current electric technology are on view: from a 1930 Detroit Electric Model 30, through the Buckeye Bullet 2.5, a racecar built by students at Ohio State University that, powered by lithium-ion batteries, reached 320 mph at the Bonneville Salt Flats in 2011.

Kingman is part of the longest continuous remaining stretch in of the original Route 66, and the Powerhouse complex contains multiple attractions for a museum visit. In addition to the auto museum, the large building contains the Kingman Visitors Center, Historic Route 66 Association of Arizona, and Route 66 Museum.

The Route 66 Electric Vehicle Museum is the creation of Roderick Wilde, the founder of the Historic Electric Vehicle Foundation. A long-time proponent of electric propulsion, Wilde started racing electric vehicles in 1993 at Phoenix International Raceway. In 1995, he and his business partner Bob Rickard built what is considered the first all-electric hot rod. The canary-yellow car, which is now in the museum, was fabricated on a 1929 Ford Roadster.

En route to the electric cars, visitors detour through the Route 66 Museum, which highlights the past of the historic road, from the early days of the National Old Trails Road up through mid-century, with a 1950 Studebaker Champion parked outside a reproduction Richfield service station. Afterwards, step down into an indoor basketball court-sized space to see the electric cars. There are 30 cars on display in relatively tight quarters, part of an ever-expanding collection that approaches 100 vehicles. One of Wilde's goals is to find larger space to showcase the entire collection.

The 1930 Detroit Electric represents "what might have been" for the future of automotive propulsion. With a top speed of 20 mph powered by 14 six-volt Edison batteries, who knows what efficiencies and technological improvements might have been achieved with greater market share and acceptance?

The Henney Kilowatt was produced in 1959 and 1960 in a partnership led by the US-based Henney Motor Company using Renault Daphines that were delivered without power trains. (Henney was previously known as a leader in the production of funeral coaches and inventor of the first electric-powered casket mover – a niche market if there ever was one.) A few dozen Kilowatts were delivered to utility companies for promotional purposes, but the line never sparked much interest. However, its transistor-based technology was a precursor to electric vehicles like GM's EV1.

One of Wilde's favorite pieces in the collection is the Custer Chair, manufactured between 1919 and 1933. As the name implies, it resembles a motorized tricycle version of a wheelchair. The model on display is a rarity, as few survived World War II scrap metal drives. Luzern Custer, a distant relation of the famous general, was a Dayton-based inventor who was inspired by his friend and business neighbor, Orville Wright. Four-wheel versions were also produced, of which Wilde says, "The Custer is the smallest street-licensed vehicle ever made. The license plate is wider than the front of the car!" Not surprisingly, many Custers were later sold as amusement park rides.

Two odd-looking cars sitting side-by-side show the evolution of the three-wheeled Personal Electric Vehicle (PEV). A Danish 1993 Citycom City El Targa had a range of 30 miles with a top speed of 35 mph. Next to it, the metallic teal Corbin Sparrow was produced in Ohio from 1999 through 2003. With an MSRP of $29,999 its range expanded to 40 miles with a top speed of 70 mph. Its curvy lines earned it the nickname the "Jelly Bean."

Although electric vehicles are all the rage today, they've been around for decades. Admittedly, the majority were primarily sold to golf courses and retirement communities. Here, golf carts are represented in style with two tricked-out versions from country music greats. Willie Nelson's 1981 Rolls-Royce themed golf cart comes complete with an on-board wet bar and crushed velvet seats with "Willie" stitched on them and sits alongside Waylon Jennings' Mercedes-Benz themed model.

The Route 66 Electric Vehicle Museums explores the possibilities of electric propulsion for the future. As recent announcements from the Big 3 automakers show, "Detroit" and "Electric" may once again be uttered in the same sentence as the technology emerges from its former role as a quirky sidecar to the mainstream automotive industry.

Route 66 Electric Vehicle Museum 120 W. Andy Devine Ave, Kingman, AZ 86401 hevf.org/route-66-ev-museum/

Braking Bad:
Celebrating the First Family of Auto Racing

Unser Racing Museum
Los Ranchos de Albuquerque, New Mexico

Long before the hit TV show *Breaking Bad* put Albuquerque, New Mexico on the television map, the city was a home to racing legends. America's First Family of Racing, the legendary Unsers, were tearing up local tracks in pursuit of speed and are celebrated here at their eponymous museum.

Four generations of the family are honored at the Unser Racing Museum in Los Ranchos de Albuquerque, just north of downtown Albuquerque. The 60+ vehicle museum, founded by Al Unser, Sr. in memory of his parents Jerry and Mary, opened in 2005 and is shaped like a wheel with each of the "spokes" representing a different aspect of Unser history, including the Pikes Peak Gallery, Indianapolis

500, Design & Engineering and Jerry's Garage, the latter a salute to family patriarch Jerry's repair shop nearby on Route 66.

It was in the original shop that the second generation of Unser boys – twins Jerry, Jr, and Louie, along with younger brothers Al and Bobby – were enthralled by stories from their racing heroes Johnnie Parsons and Tony Bettenhausen, who stopped by before heading to their next competition.

Upon entering the museum, the first thing visitors notice is a spot lit bright yellow #25 racing car spinning on a turntable at the hub of the museum. With its gleaming presence it wouldn't look out of place as a shiny bauble at the Paris Motor Show. Built by March Race Cars of England in 1986 as a Model C, its double overhead cam Cosworth turbocharged 159 cubic inch V8 engine reached 850 horsepower. It's a teammate of the car that a 47-year-old Al, Senior drove to victory in the 1987 Indy 500 as a last-minute replacement for Danny Ongais. (Last time I toured the Penske Museum in Phoenix the actual race winner was on display there.)

Prior to their fame at the Brickyard, Unser racing success went back decades. The family started more humbly as kings of the hill – literally – with the Pikes Peak Hill Climb in Colorado. In 1934 Louis Unser, driving a Stutz Special, won his first climb at Pikes Peak. He went on to win five in a row of a total of nine victories as Unsers dominated the race. The museum displays a host of cars and memorabilia related to what became the family racing event. Three generations of Unsers – Louis, Bobby, Al, Al Junior, and Robby – have won that race more than two dozen times.

Car #58, in which Bobby won Pikes Peak for the first of his 10 victories (the last in 1986 at the relatively advanced age of 52), is on display. Engineered and built by his dad, Jerry Senior, in his shop on Route 66, it's powered by a one-of-a-kind Jaguar 4-liter, 6-cylinder engine with a 4-speed Jaguar transmission fueled by methanol.

The latest addition to the museum is a separate building out back that holds Al, Senior's 35-vehicle antique car collection along with room upon room festooned with enough Unser championship trophies, plaques and racing memorabilia, including championship jackets and scuffed race-worn helmets, to sink a small battleship.

A 1946 Chevrolet Business Coupe is loaded with a 3-speed manual transmission with vacuum assisted shifting, coil spring independent front suspension, live rear axle with semi-elliptical leaf springs and 4 wheel hydraulically actuated drum brakes. Next to it, a ½-ton 1941 Chevy Pickup Truck looks odd because only one half of the split windshield has a wiper dangling from the roof; at the time it was an option to have a second windshield wiper for the passenger.

Two Indy 500 pace cars here – a 1970 Oldsmobile 442 and 1987 Chrysler Le Baron – were awarded to Al, Senior after winning those races.

But the Unsers aren't just a Pikes Peak and Indy 500 racing family. Other cars here show the breadth of their racing experience including: the Johnny Lightning car in which Al, Sr. dominated the dirt track circuit in 1970; a hot pink 1994 Dodge Avenger dubbed "The Pink Panther" that Al, Jr. drove to victory in a 1994 IROC race at the Michigan Speedway; and a 2001 Legends car, Legends cars are 5/8 scale fiberglass versions of famed NASCAR modifieds.

But what does a famous racer drive when he's not tearing around an oval track? Al Senior's "Sunday Driver" is here too. It's a reproduction 1966 Ford Cobra built in a limited edition in 1994 by Excalibur Motor Company of Milwaukee. In the parking lot don't miss the Jersey barrier that Al crashed into at the 1989 Indy 500. Fortunately, he wasn't driving the Cobra that day.

The legacy of the Unser family on American racing is truly unique. Although 2021 was a tough year for the Unser family with the deaths of Bobby Senior and Junior, plus Al Unser Sr. in December, fortunately the memories and their impact on racing live on at this museum.

Unser Racing Museum 1776 Montaño Road NW, Los Ranchos de Albuquerque, NM 87107
www.UnserRacingMuseum.com

There's a neighborhood in Albuquerque with street names to appeal to the classic car afficionado including Durant Avenue, Hupmobile Road, Pierce Arrow Road, Stutz Drive, Willys Knight Drive and (the relatively obscure) Jewett Ave. It's located about a mile and half north of historic Route 66, which in Albuquerque is the longest urban stretch of the Mother Road. Alas, the only classic we spotted while driving through was a 1970's era Datsun B210 parked on the street. Perhaps the Hupmobiles and Stutzes are behind garage doors.

War Eagles Fly Over the Desert:
A Unique Museum Combines Classic Automobiles and Vintage Military Aircraft

War Eagles Air Museum Santa Teresa, New Mexico

The War Eagles Air Museum, on the outskirts of El Paso, Texas, contains a varied assemblage of airplanes, along with classic automobiles tucked under their wings. Most of the three-dozen aircraft are veterans of the armed forces – serving in World War II, Korea and Vietnam for the United States, Great Britain, Germany, and the Soviet Union – while the 50+ domestic and imported cars represent a mix of civilian and military uses.

The collection is housed in a hangar at Dona Aña County Airport, in the desert town of Santa Teresa, New Mexico, just six miles north of the US-Mexico border. The mid-century ambiance of crooners Nat "King" Cole and Bing Crosby piped in over the speakers is punctuated by the occasional rumble of a propeller as airplanes taxi nearby for takeoff. Many of the aircraft in the museum can still fly; your visit might include one of them being fired up and taken out for a test flight.

The museum was founded in 1989 as a center for aviation history by West Texas rancher and oilman John T. MacGuire and his wife Betty, who were both pilots. With the donation of foreign-made automobiles and motorcycles by local Glenn Hoidale, the museum became an automotive destination as well.

The North American TF-51D Mustang of World War II acclaim is a rarity as it is a two-seat version of the fabled fighter. Dubbed the "Friendly Ghost," it's the result of a 1956 project by the Texas Engineering & Manufacturing Corporation (TEMCO) to convert 15 World War II-era Mustang fighter planes into dual-control trainers. This plane was spotted in parts in a salvage yard in Jakarta, Indonesia in the 1970s. After years of restoration work, it was brought to the museum and flown by the MacGuires.

One of the unique aspects of the museum is seeing cars and airplanes side-by-side, which allows for some clever combinations. Accordingly, parked next to the flying Mustang is a similarly sleek 1966 Ford Mustang convertible in an appropriate sky-blue color, creating a tableau not often seen.

The museum's C-47A flew in World War II, arriving in England in May 1944 as part of the IX Troop Carrier Command of the 9th Air Force. After flying paratroopers on D-Day, it was converted to a DC-3C for civilian use when its wartime service ended. Parked beneath it is a 1942 Cadillac coupe – it represents one of the last vestiges of American automobile manufacturing before the United States entered the war and rapidly converted its civilian industrial capacity to military production.

Produced late in the first year of operations, the distinctive yellow 1937 Piper J-3 Cub is just the 42nd of this iconic airplane produced, and likely the world's oldest operational Piper aircraft. It sits next to a 1914 Ford Model T speedster. Per museum Executive Director Bob Dockendorf, "Ford didn't make a speedster. It's an example of neighborhood hot rods built by teenagers taking parts from a Model A, parts from a Model T and parts from anything else they might find laying around."

With painted flames roaring up its hood, a 1931 Ford Model A Roadster, another example of hot rod culture, is outfitted with a 1949 239 ci flathead engine, which is paired with a 1945 North American AT-6F Texan. The Texan was produced by the thousands to provide training to many American pilots during World War II; in the UK the Royal Air Force used a version of the same aircraft, designated the Harvard.

The influence of the UK's Royal Observer Corps is seen in the collection of hand-held scale models that were used to train Allied military personnel in aircraft identification, a skill that saved countless lives during the war.

Cold War-era jet aircraft include a Soviet-built MiG-15 trainer (designated by NATO as the *Midget*), a MiG-21 fighter that served in the East German Air Force and a North American FJ-2 Fury.

There are also two rows of vehicles ranging from a pair of 1950 and 1951 Ford pickup trucks to international cars like a 1965 Volvo 122S, pumpkin-colored 1972 Honda 600 and a 1973 Honda Civic. The latter are examples of daily drivers not often found in museums. The Honda 600 represented the company's first foray into the American automotive market. A 1958 Morris Minor 1000 rounds out the tableau of "regular" cars.

Military vehicles complete the automotive section, including a US Navy M37 ¾-ton truck, 1952 Willys Jeep M-38 in Marine Corps markings, and a US Army 1952 Willys Jeep M-38 liveried as a Military Police vehicle. The automobilia collection also includes a wide array of vintage gas pumps.

This was our second visit to the museum. On our first trip, four years earlier, we met a local man named Maynard Beamesderfer, who was a war eagle himself. Known as "Beamy," he was a D-Day veteran who, as a 19-year-old, parachuted into Normandy the night before the invasion as part of the Pathfinders of the 101st Airborne Screaming Eagles, flying over in a C-47 just like the one on display.

Beamy passed away before this visit, but his legacy lives on with two motorized scooters that disabled visitors can use to traverse the museum – they are aptly labeled "Beamy 1" and Beamy 2."

With its interesting mix of displays, the War Eagles Air Museum is a fascinating destination for anyone interested in classic cars and military aircraft.

War Eagles Air Museum 8012 Airport Road, Santa Teresa, NM 88008

www.WarEaglesAirMuseum.com

Wheels in the Sky in Oregon

Western Antique Aeroplane & Automobile Museum Hood River, Oregon

There is a near universal truism in the genesis of automotive museums. They usually start with someone's interest in cars. That interest gradually grows into a hobby, then an obsession, then a collection. When space finally runs out at home, that collection finds a home of its own and becomes a museum. Most of us stop at the hobby stage but for a select few that's just not enough.

For Terry Brandt, the steps got even more complicated because he was interested in cars AND airplanes, plus assorted military vehicles and motorcycles. Eventually he reached a crossroads when his wife Lois told him he was either going to sell the collection or start a museum. He chose the latter, creating the Western Antique

Aeroplane & Automobile Museum (WAAAM) two miles south of the Columbia River in Hood River, Oregon.

When the museum opened in 2007 there were 42 airplanes and just a handful of automobiles. Now there are more than 130 vehicles plus 75 aircraft sprawling across 2.5 acres of indoor hangar space that looks large enough to hold the Goodyear blimp with room to spare.

Almost all the aircraft on display have been donated to the museum by community members. About half of the cars have been donated; the remainder are either due to be donated or on loan.

WAAAM is a "living museum," where most of the vehicles and aircraft still operate as often as possible. It's located adjacent to Ken Jernstedt Airfield, named after a pilot who flew with the Flying Tigers in the Pacific during World War II.

Brandt himself grew up in an aviation-oriented family. His parents were the Fixed Base Operators of an airport in Maryville, California and he learned to fly at the tender age of twelve. The 1938 J-3 Cub he bought a few years later launched a half century of collecting.

EARTH

The selection is certainly eclectic. Vehicle variety ranges from a 1900 Locomobile Steam Car Runabout through a rare 1927 Moon Brougham to a one-cylinder 1981 HMV Freeway microcar that could achieve 100 mpg. Despite the freeway moniker though, I think I'd stick to local roads in this one.

In one corner visitors will find a 1941 Packard Model 120 parked next to a 1981 Avanti II. What? Didn't Avanti production stop in the '60s? After the demise of Studebaker, former dealers Leo Newman and Nate & Arnold Altman from South Bend, Indiana picked up the torch and started producing the Avanti II.

The 1920 Buick 2-door Country Club Coupe exudes elegance. Buick had retooled the line and started its reputation for chrome with this model. Move forward nearly a half-century to one of my favorite cars: a 1965 Buick Riviera in either Seafoam Green or Champagne Mist. (After all these years I can never tell them apart.) Phil and Judy Jensen, who donated 19 cars to the museum, say the Riviera is their favorite too. The generous Jensens also donated the gorgeous 1950 Kaiser Virginian hardtop convertible in its original "Indian Ceramic" color that's a vibrant blend of salmon and coral.

Trucks on display include a 1914 Ford Model T Depot Hack, 1917 Federal Flatbed, 1925 Autocar Truck, 1933 International Pickup Truck, and a 1953 Chevrolet Tank Truck.

WIND

Although Brandt loves classic cars, since his first love was airplanes the collection here is very select. The heart of the collection is from the 1920s through the 1940s and features names such as Stearman, Curtiss Wright, Monocoupe, Waco, Piper Cub, Stinson and many more. The aircraft have been painstakingly restored and, best of all, they still fly.

Rarities include a 1928 Boeing 40C biplane that is the oldest Boeing airplane still flying; a 1928 WACO ATO Taperwing that was a popular stunt plane; and a 1929 St. Louis Cardinal C-2 that was built by the aviation subsidiary of a trolley car company.

The 1933 WACO UIC 4-seat cabin biplane, one of 83 that were built, is powered by a Continental R-670, 220 HP engine. The interior is luxuriously fit out with upholstery, full flight and engine instruments, automobile type doors on both sides, individual front seats, and a roomy bench seat for two in the rear. The WACO was popular with famous names like aviation pioneer Jacqueline Cochran, who was the first woman to break the sound barrier. A scale model of the biplane sits in the shadow of its left wing.

FIRE

The military collection is comprised of two dozen aircraft including a 1917 Curtiss JN-4D Jenny (of postage stamp fame); a 1940 Naval

Aircraft Factory N3N-3 that was the last operational biplane in the US armed forces; and a 1943 Piper HE-1 air ambulance.

Military vehicles include a 1919 Ford Model T ambulance; 1939 White M3A1 Scout Car; and a World War II Studebaker M29C cargo carrier.

The Western Antique Aeroplane & Automobile Museum also includes gliders, motorcycles, tractors, and bicycles. A rare, sidecar motorized bicycle is the one-off Champ-Cycle created in 1943 by Oregonian Champ Bond. He mated a circa early 1940s Wards Hawthorne bicycle with a ½ hp Briggs and Stratton engine borrowed from a washing machine and then added a sidecar so his kids would have transportation to a one-room school that was located a few miles away.

Since this is very much a living museum, events include Second Saturdays where visitors can ride in the cars and watch the vintage aircraft take off and land at the adjacent runway. The Traffic Jam, car show and more, takes place in July. The weekend after Labor Day is the Annual Hood River Fly-In with hundreds of colorful classic planes taking part. During WAAAM Camp in the summer kids get hands-on experience learning about early aviation and automobiles. Model T driving classes take place throughout the year but fill up early. In the Decades Driving School you'll get to drive cars from the '30s, '40s, and '50s.

Western Antique Aeroplane & Automobile Museum 1600 Air Museum Road, Hood River, OR 97031

www.waaamuseum.org

Getting Taken for a Ride in California

Zimmerman Automobile Driving Museum
El Segundo, California

NOTE: When this article was originally published, the museum was called the Automobile Driving Museum. After co-founder Stanley Zimmerman passed away in 2020 the museum was renamed.

Let's say you wanted to go out for a Sunday drive in a 1929 Ford Model A Fire Chief car or a 1956 Plymouth Belvedere or, if your tastes are sportier, a 1971 AMC Javelin AMX. Well, you'd have to own a pretty selective personal car collection to do that. Or you could visit the Automobile Driving Museum in El Segundo, California that bills itself as "the museum that takes you for a ride." Every Sunday they select three to four cars out of the collection of antique, vintage and muscle cars and take visitors for short journeys on local city streets, less than a mile from Los Angeles International Airport.

The museum was founded by friends Stanley Zimmerman and Earl Rubenstein. In 1971, they attended a car show but were put off by all the signs that said, "Don't Touch." As Zimmerman recalls, "We wanted to open a museum someday where people could sit in the cars and also go for rides." They felt visitors should experience the cars, hear their engines rumble and feel the same joy that he's had since he started driving at 12 (!) years of age. Hence, the reason for the Sunday Rides.

The 130-car collection ranges from a 1909 Ford Model T to a 1989 Porsche 911 Speedster. It's primarily focused on cars that were people's daily drivers like a 1962 Chevrolet Corvair or a 1965 Studebaker Wagonaire station wagon. On our tour of the museum, Zimmerman was an enthusiastic guide whose love for classic cars is only surpassed by his love of seeing people enjoying them.

One of the unique facets here is the lack of ropes or barriers around the cars – they are also set up far enough apart so people can open the doors and climb in. That's why it's considered the "petting zoo" of car museums. As an exception, a few priceless cars like a 1930 Stutz Monte Carlo Sedan (one of three built with a fabric wrapped body), a 1937 Pierce-Arrow Town Car and a 1936 Packard Dietrich convertible are set up in a separate area that looks like an upscale circa 1920s automobile showroom. However, visitors may still enter this area to view the cars up close.

The 1936 Packard was Zimmerman's first foray into classic cars, a painful experience he recalls well. According to Zimmerman, "I wanted to buy a car that needed extensive restoration and do all the work. I found this car that needed everything. It was the stupidest thing I ever did. It took 30 years to restore because of all the mistakes I made. My advice now is to buy a car that's already restored."

A bevy of British beauties highlights the sporty cars that American servicemen American returning from World War II were first exposed to during their time in Great Britain and now wanted to see parked in their own driveways. Left-hand drive versions here include a 1952 MG TD Roadster, 1956 Morgan Plus Roadster and a 1959 Austin-Healey 3000 that *Road & Track* magazine called "dollar for dollar one of the top sports cars in the world."

One of the benefits of being allowed to sit in the cars was learning that twisting my body in and out of that 1956 Morgan I've always pined for was an ordeal akin to human origami, something I wouldn't have known just by looking at it behind velvet ropes.

One car here that I remember well from my youth, but have never seen in a museum, is a 1975 AMC Pacer – however, the oft-maligned vehicle deserves some recognition. The "greenhouse on wheels" featured acres of glass, a cab-forward design and, despite its small size, enough elbow room for a passel of clowns who would look right at home riding in it as a circus attraction. Marketed as the "first wide small car," there's no denying that it stands out as a unique product from Detroit and is remembered more than most of its ho-hum contemporaries.

Another quirky car is the 1963 Studebaker Avanti. Although the fiber-glass bodied speed machine with a supercharged 240 hp V8 set several records at the Bonneville Salt Flats, its quirky asymmetric styling was a bit too far out for mainstream American tastes.

Part of the museum's mission is to attract the next generation of car collectors to the hobby. Activities for youngsters include the monthly Hot Wheels Garage events for kids aged 10 and under where they race small cars and participate in hands-on automotive activities: the reward for completing all their tasks is a free Hot Wheel car. There's also a project for local secondary school students who are restoring a 1966 Amphicar.

After a spin in one of the museum's cars, it's tempting to move to sunny California and become one of the volunteers who gets to hop into a classic car and, every Sunday, take visitors for a ride.

Zimmerman Automobile Driving Museum 610 Lairport Street, El Segundo, CA 90245 www.AutomobileDrivingMuseum.org

Interviews

In The Garage With Jay Leno

For more than 20 years, America invited Jay Leno into their homes via his hosting of The Tonight Show. These days, the comedian returns the favor by welcoming viewers to experience his California-based car collection on the popular CNBC television show Jay Leno's Garage. For all his years of late-night hosting and stand-up comedy, his true passion has always been cars and motorcycles. During the show, Jay's good-natured personality is on full display as he highlights his assemblage of more than 150 rare and exotic automobiles from around the globe. But Jay doesn't believe in treating his cars as mere precious baubles that can't be touched; they're meant to rumble and rumble he does as he takes them out for a spin on city streets, inviting the audience along for a vicarious ride.

We caught up with Jay during a break from filming new episodes and learned more about his passion for automobiles, and his take on the classic car hobby today.

Michael Milne: What was it like growing up as a car buff in your family?

Jay Leno: When I was 16, I went with my parents when they were buying a 1966 Ford Galaxie. The dealer was out of stock but I convinced my dad to order one and asked if I could pick the engine. My mother said, "Oh let the boy pick it. What difference does it make?" I pulled the salesman aside and said, "We want the 428-cubic-inch 7-Liter motor with the police pursuit package and the muffler delete option." A month later when we picked up the car my dad started the engine and it roared: "HUM-UHNA, HUM-UHNA, HUM-UHNA." He started screaming that there's a hole in the muffler. The salesman explained that a muffler doesn't come with the police pursuit package. Well, now my dad knows he's been had and is shooting knife stares at me. He didn't speak to me for a month. But some time later I was in my parents' room and I noticed he had a speeding ticket for going 110 miles an hour. The car actually made him the coolest guy in the insurance office where he worked.

MM: What was your first car?

JL: When I was 14-years-old I found a '34 Ford pickup for sale at a gas station in Reading, Massachusetts. I bought it with the money I made working and my dad helped out a bit. We dragged it home and, after I got it running, I practiced going up and down the driveway for two years until I earned my license.

MM: What types of cars would be a good entryway for someone into the classic car hobby?

JL: I predict the Mazda Miata will be the Mustang of 2025 because the first generation was easy to work on and they were pretty cool cars. Plus, they sold a million of them so there are plenty out there. An exotic collectible that's cheap is a 1960s Chevy Corvair. Here was the first truly European style American car that really was the American Porsche. [Among the shared features was a rear-mounted, air-cooled engine.] It was revolutionary at the time.

MM: The Corvair gained some notoriety when it was mentioned in Ralph Nader's 1965 book Unsafe At Any Speed. Was Ralph Nader wrong about the car?

JL: When the book first came out it didn't focus on the Corvair. The book focused on Volkswagen. The Corvair was just a chapter. In fact, there was a National Highway Traffic Safety Administration study in the early '70s that determined the Corvair was no more dangerous or safe than any other production car in America. But Ralph Nader has done a lot of good. I mean accidents you walk away from now would have killed you in 1965. So that's an improvement.

MM: If you had to pick one of your cars for a cross-country road trip, which would it be?

JL: I had two younger guys call me and they said, "Mr. Leno, we're driving cross-country in an antique car. We're leaving New York City on Thursday and we hope to be in LA next week, can we stop by your garage as the final place?"

I said, "Sure. You're driving an antique car? Cool, cool. What kind of antique car are you driving?"

"A '68 Cadillac."

I told them, "My father did that trip like 50 times. Okay? You've got air conditioning, you've got AM-FM, and you've got electric seats." But to them it was an antique car! It's 50 years old. I think they're going to say something like a Model T. No, they're going cross-country in a '68 Cadillac. It just made me laugh.

But what car would I pick? I'd say one of the Duesenbergs, because that's one of the few truly classic cars you can drive at 80 or 90 miles per hour all day long on the freeway without having a problem with it.

MM: What is your wife Mavis's involvement in your car collection?

JL: She doesn't get involved in it, but at least she knows where I am. When you come home reeking of transmission fluid they know you're not out fooling around. I've never really thought of my stuff as a collection, I just never sold anything. All my cars are registered and I drive them all.

MM: In the age of Uber and self-driving cars, what do you see as the future of the car hobby?

JL: I find that fewer young people are interested in cars but the ones who are know way more than we did at their age. I'm astounded when I get some of these eighteen-year-old technicians in here and they know how to work on everything. I just think it changes. It's like Mark Twain said, "I like progress, it's change I don't like." So, I'm optimistic about the hobby.

On the Road with Alice Cooper

Rock-and-Roll Hall-of-Famer Alice Cooper has achieved legendary status for his many hits like School's Out and No More Mr. Nice Guy. He still tours for almost 200 days annually, with performances that are part vaudeville, part Broadway, and 100% musical thunder. In keeping with his macabre on-stage persona, he slides into a guillotine for the highlight of the show. Shocking yes, but all done with a sly wink at the audience. Off stage Cooper is a reflective family man with many interests, including classic cars and his foundation, Solid Rock, that helps teens explore and develop their artistic talents in his hometown of Phoenix.

Michael Milne: How did you first get interested in cars?

Alice Cooper: I'm originally from Detroit so it's in my DNA. I'd always sit in art class designing cars. In my teens I was at that perfect age, with all the Beach Boys songs about cars and driving. A car was your declaration of independence that also reflected who you were. You had to have something that was flashy and cool.

MM: What was your first car?

AC: It was a 1966 Ford Fairlane GT 390, yellow with a black stripe. The band was starting to make some money while I was in high school, so my share went into a drawer. After two years I had enough to buy it new. By this time my family had moved to Phoenix because of my asthma, so my friends and I would drive out into the desert and cut loose.

MM: You mentioned cars being in your DNA?

AC My dad sold used cars on Woodward Avenue in Detroit. Unfortunately for him, he was an honest used car salesman. He would point out if the odometer had been turned back or if the car had been in an accident, so he made no money at it. When that didn't work out he ended up selling new Plymouths, so we'd get a Plymouth Fury every year, watching as the tail fins grew larger and larger. By 1958 it was a battleship.

MM: What's a car that you pined for in your youth that you now own?

AC: The 1963 Studebaker Avanti. People hated how the car looked, but I liked it because it's got this asymmetrical body and was just the weirdest car. When it came out, I was 15 and thought it was the coolest thing I'd ever seen in my life. According to an FBI agent that I later met, the one I own was being driven by a Soviet spy when that agent arrested him, so I'll have to hold on to that one.

MM: With a rigorous touring schedule, what are some tips for staying sane on the road?

AC: Travel with people you like to spend time with. For the band I pick musicians I like, they all get along, and they're professionals. I play golf every morning; nine holes if there's a concert or eighteen if it's an off night. My wife Sheryl, to whom I've been married for 43 years, is a dancer in the show and travels with us, so I bring "home" with me.

MM: What's an item you always travel with?

AC: It sounds crazy, but I always bring kung fu video tapes. I try to find obscure films like Five Golden Shaolins vs. The Army of Darkness. There are thousands of them out there. The dubbing is really bad, but the fight scenes are great, and they get me charged up for the show. Before I go on stage, I watch an hour of these.

MM: How did the Solid Rock Teen Center get started?

AC: While visiting a neighborhood ministry program in a gangland part of town I saw two sixteen-year-old kids doing a drug deal on the street. I thought, 'How does that kid not know he might be the best guitar player in Arizona, while the other kid might be the best drummer?' I thought we could run a program, just for teenagers, where they would come in and learn any instrument for free. Gang kids or the richest kid in Paradise Valley, what do they have in common? Music.

We've expanded from music performance to art and dance. We tell kids 'Come in and discover your talent and let us help you nurture it.' We get 100 kids a day here, from all walks of life, who come because they are going to get something out of it that could change their life. Our first in-house competition was won by Jordin Sparks. When she went on to win American Idol in 2007, she wore her Solid Rock bracelet the whole time.

INDEX

AACA Museum, US   89
Alfa Romeo Historical Museum, Italy   36
America's Packard Museum, US   99
Auburn Cord Duesenberg Automobile Museum, US   145

Boyertown Museum of Historic Vehicles, US   93

Cars of Socialism Museum, Bulgaria   1
Cité de' L'Automobile, France   6
Classic Motor Museum, US   96
Collezione Umberto Panini Motor Museum, Italy   48
Crawford Auto Aviation Collection, US   99
Cussler Museum, US   192

Dr. Carl Benz Auto Museum, Germany   17

Early Ford V8 Foundation & Museum, US   145
Edge Motor Museum, US   173
Enzo Ferrari Museum, Italy   48

Ferrari Museum, Italy   48
Fiat Museum, Italy   40
Ford Piquette Avenue Plant, US   103
Franklin Auto Museum, US   196
Frick Car & Carriage Museum, US   107

Gasoline Alley, Canada   80
Gilmore Car Museum, US   110

Haynes International Motor Museum, UK   64
Hellenic Motor Museum, Greece   33
Henry Ford Museum of American Innovation, US   114
Heritage Museums & Gardens, US   117

Indianapolis Motor Speedway Museum, US   150

Jim's Vintage Garages, Canada   85

Keystone Truck & Tractor Museum, US   120

Lamborghini Museum, Italy   48
Lane Motor Museum, US   153
LeMay – America's Car Museum, US   199
LeMay Family Collection, US   199
London Bus Museum at Brooklands, UK   67
London Transport Museum, UK   67

Manitoba Antique Automobile Museum, Canada   85
Manoir de'l'Automobile, France   9
Mercedes-Benz Museum, Germany   20
Midwest Dream Car Collection, US   158
Midwest Microcar Museum, US   162
Mullin Automobile Museum, US   204
Murphy Auto Museum, US   204
Museo Enzo Ferrari, Italy   48
Museo Ferrari, Italy   48
Museo Lamborghini, Italy   48
Museum of Municipal Engineering, Poland   54

National Auto & Truck Museum, US   145
National Auto Museum, Italy   44
National Automobile Museum, US   209
National Corvette Museum, US   166
National Museum of the United States Army, US   124
National Motor Museum at Beaulieu, UK   71
National Museum of Scotland, UK   74
National Packard Museum, US   99

Petersen Automotive Museum, US   213

Pontiac-Oakland Museum, US   170
Porsche Museum, Germany   23
Presley Motors at Graceland, US   173

Rambler Ranch, US   217
Riverside Museum, UK   74
Route 66 Electric Vehicle Museum, US   221

Shelby Heritage Center, US   209
Simeone Foundation Automotive Museum, US   129
Skoda Museum, Denmark   4
Speedwell Museum of American Speed, US   176
Stahl's Automotive Foundation, US   180
State Police Car Museum, Italy   51
Studebaker National Museum, US   184

Tampa Bay Automobile Museum, US   134
Technical Museum of Slovenia, Slovenia   61
Technik Museums Sinsheim, Germany   26
Technik Museums Speyer, Germany   26
Tiriac Collection, Romania   58
Trabi Museum, Germany   30
24 Hours of Le Mans Museum, France   13

Umberto Panini Museum, Italy   48
Unser Racing Museum, US   224
US Army Transportation Museum, US   138

War Eagles Air Museum, US   228
Western Antique Aeroplane & Automobile Museum, US   232
Wheels of Yesteryear, US   142
Wisconsin Automobile Museum, US   188

Zimmerman Automobile Driving Museum, US   236

ABOUT THE AUTHOR

Classic car and travel writer Michael Milne has loved driving since he operated his first pedal car as a toddler in Ohio.

He writes about car museums and road trips for *Hemmings Motor News, AAA World, Philadelphia Inquirer, Octane, Classic Military Vehicle*, and many other publications.

Hemmings Motor News Radio calls Milne the "Rick Steves of car museums."

He and his ever-patient wife Larissa spent two years on an epic American road trip driving coast-to-coast to research the *Roadster Guide to America's Classic Car Museums & Attractions*.

They are the co-authors of *Philadelphia Liberty Trail: Trace the Path of America's Heritage*, that takes a revolutionary approach to the city's historic district. Full-time global nomads since 2011, they write about their journey at www.ChangesInLongitude.com.

www.ingramcontent.com/pod-product-compliance
Lightning Source LLC
Chambersburg PA
CBHW031244090426
42742CB00007B/307